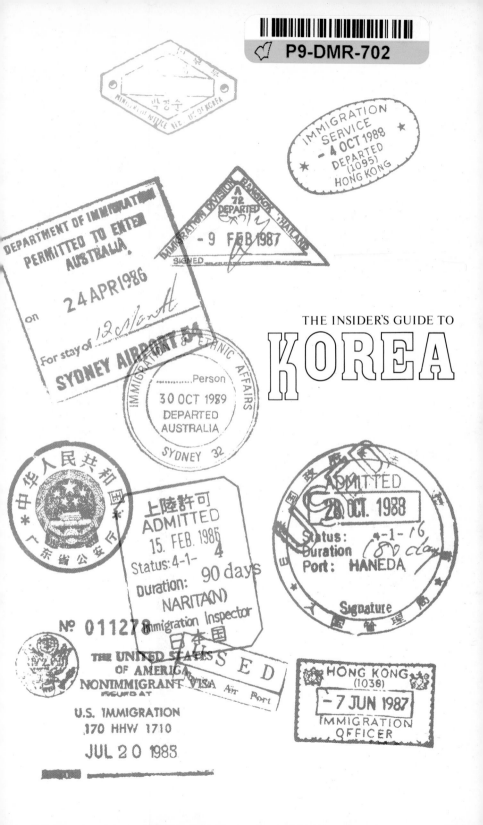

THE INSIDER'S GUIDE TO

KOREA

THE INSIDER'S GUIDES
JAPAN • CHINA • KOREA • HAWAII • HONG KONG • AUSTRALIA
THAILAND* • BALI* • MEXICO* • INDIA*

The Insider's Guide to Korea
First published 1987
Seoul International Publishing House
Yongdong P.O. Box 629, Seoul, Korea
Tel 543-6010, 542-9308

© 1987 CFW Publications Ltd

ISBN: 962 7031 18 6

Created, edited and produced by CFW Publications Ltd
Editor in Chief: Allan Amsel
Design: Hon Bing-wah/Kinggraphic
Text and artwork composed and information updated
on an NBI System 5000 computer

ACKNOWLEDGMENTS
The author would like to thank Chun Shil Adams
of Seoul International Publishing House and the Korea National
Tourism Corporation for helping in various ways with the factual
information contained in this guidebook.

In preparation

Printed in Korea

THE INSIDER'S GUIDE TO
KOREA

by Peter Popham

Photographed by Alain Evrard

SEOUL INTERNATIONAL PUBLISHING HOUSE
Seoul

Contents

KOREA

U.S.S.R.

Beijing

KOREA

JAPAN
Tokyo

Shanghai

CHINA

Guangzhou

TAIWAN

HONG KONG

PACIFIC
OCEAN

THE PHILIPPINES

YELLOW

Mokp'o

Chindo

CHEJU-DO

Cheju

Songsan

Halim   *Hallasan*

Sogwip'o

Taejong

N

Railways

Roads

50km

Hon

Korea: The Hermit Emerges

KOREA TODAY

For the traveler, Korea is a country whose time has come. A flash-point of the cold war, a political embarrassment, a store-house of bitter memories, a sort of second-rate Japan without the charm - these are the negative terms in which the Republic of Korea has customarily been considered and dismissed. The reality, however, has always been much more interesting. Korea is a country with a powerful identity of its own. A

good neighbor to China, a beneficiary over the millennia of all the wealth of Chinese cultural achievement, it has never failed to interpret these gifts in own way, infusing them with flavors found nowhere else. There is nothing in the world, for instance, like Korean food, or classical Korean pottery, or modern Korean dance. Like the Irish, to whom they are sometimes compared, centuries of oppression have done nothing to subdue these people: the crucible of hardship has fused their identity into something tough and distinctive. Even more remarkably, their troubles have failed to rob them of their humanity. Straphanging on the Seoul subway, the visitor is taken aback to find his heavy bag taken from him - not by a thief, but by a seated passenger, happy to relieve him of the weight for a few stops. In

city and country alike, disinterested kindness and hospitality are found everywhere. Honesty is universal.

Travelers attracted by Korea's heritage will find all manner of things to absorb them, from mountain temples to city palaces, from villages unchanged for centuries to the tombs of kings who died fifteen hundred or more years ago. But even for those who just want a holiday, Korea has a lot to offer: the wooded mountains of the numerous national parks, excellent beaches, the voluptuously beautiful island of Cheju-do in the south, which has almost everything and is quite unspoiled. Seoul, a crazy shambles just a year or two back when they were building the subway, is now much calmer and can be negotiated with ease. Its covered markets with their hundreds of little eateries offer an incredible banquet for the senses, even if you don't eat anything. And for high-quality clothes, shoes and bags, the city remains the bargain basement of the world.

The history of Korea is deeply sad, a bitter saga of wars and invasions, and the worst is not over yet. The slicing of the country into two hostile states, still effectively at war with each other more than thirty years after the end of hostilities, is a situation no Korean can resign himself to happily. But with economic success, and the international recognition symbolized by the decision to stage the 1988 Olympics in the country, the Republic is riding a wave of self-confidence, and part of that is seen in the welcome they offer visitors. First-class hotels are abundant in Seoul, Kyongju, Pusan, and Cheju-do, while simpler accommodation is obtainable at every fork in the road. New expressways augment the punctual and comfortable trains and the dense network of fast and frequent (though somewhat

ABOVE Traditional houses in Seoul's Pangsang-dong section, tightly nested together and RIGHT a more spacious feeling created in the striking architecture of Kyobo Building in the city's Chongjin-dong district.

hair-raising) buses: a self-propelled vacation in Korea is now a real possibility, and will become an even more useful one when rent-a-car facilities are expanded. The Korea National Tourism Corporation has an elaborate information office in the center of Seoul, and an impressive array of well-produced literature in English. People continue to assert that *han' gul*, the Korean writing system, is one of the world's easiest alphabets (and it's true that it's not difficult), but the realization that most visitors to the Olympics are unlikely to go to the trouble of learning it is slowly sinking in, and more and more restaurants are investing in romanized menus.

Once known as the Hermit Kingdom on account of its introspective ways, Korea has emerged into the strong light of international curiosity, and it's looking good: compact, cheap, easily traveled, lots of fun. Its women are beautiful. It's a sheer holiday, and an education in history, culture and human resilience, rolled into one.

"THE COUNTRY THAT STANDS ON END"

Roughly forty million people live in the Republic of Korea which, with an area of 99,000 sq km (38,224 sq miles), is smaller than the communist north, 122,000 sq km (47,104 sq miles). The peninsula as a whole is comparable in size to Great Britain or New York State. Located between 43 degrees and 34 degrees north, it stretches 1,000 km (620 miles) from north to south and 216 km (134 miles) from east to west at its narrowest point. To the west lie the Yellow Sea and China, to the east the East Sea (Sea of Japan) and the southwest extreme of the Japanese archipelago. Scattered along the rugged coastline are over three thousand islands.

Korea is a land of mountains, and wherever you are, even in central

Seoul, the skyline is bounded by low but craggy peaks, ridge upon ridge of them. So ubiquitous are they that Korea has been nicknamed "the country that stands on end." The spaces in between devoted to agriculture and industry, well watered by the short, twisting, fast-flowing rivers, constitute just twenty per cent of the total area.

Though it's hard to appreciate the fact while traveling through the country, the whole peninsula is on a tilt, the highest peaks being in the east of the country and sloping erratically to lower

land in the west. On the east coast the magnificent Diamond Mountains drop precipitously to the sea, where fishing coves alternate with sandy beaches. The west coast is riddled with shallow, narrow inlets where tidal changes, amounting in some places to twenty-five feet, are among the most extreme in the world. The many islands off this coast are the peaks of long-submerged mountains.

Though ravaged by the civil war, the Korean countryside is once again rich in colorful flora and exotic fauna. The mountains, many of them stripped almost bare of vegetation at one time (some blame the greedy Japanese colonizers, others say they were decimated by the demand for fuel for the *ondol* under-floor heating systems), have been intensively reforested with trees native to the peninsula such as pine and juniper, maple and cherry. Nowadays it would take a very keen eye to spot

signs of past damage.

Much effort has also been thrown into conserving the country's wildlife, and today you'll see egrets and herons feeding in the paddies, pheasants and magpies in the bushes, kingfishers, woodpeckers and hoopoes perching in the trees. In one of the weirdest of the many ironies of the civil war's aftermath, the no-man's-land along the 38th parallel, the so-called Demilitarized Zone (DMZ), uncultivated for thirty years and more, has become quite accidentally a nature reserve where among other endangered species the splendid Manchurian crane, a symbol of longevity throughout the East with its snow-white plumage, red feather cap and black-trimmed wings, takes refuge from the folly of mankind.

CLIMATE

Korea has a temperate continental climate with four distinct seasons. It is affected by both the bitter cold fronts which reach down from Siberia in the north, and the annual monsoon rains of the Pacific region to the south, which drench the country in late June and July. Winters are cold and dry, though the whole country also receives a fair amount of snow, even Cheju-do island far to the south, which is so mild for most of the year that it does without *ondol*. Winters in the Republic are naturally less severe than in the north, though only Eskimos would deliberately choose to visit in this season. Summers by contrast are hot and humid everywhere, with temperatures rising to 37°C (98°F).

Unquestionably the best seasons to visit the country are spring and autumn, when the days are warm and balmy, the nights crisp and cool, and the countryside, whether bright with blossoms or fiery with autumn leaves, looks its best and most ravishing.

A TURBULENT HISTORY

THE FIRST THREE THOUSAND YEARS

The ancestors of the present-day Korean people were migrant tribes, cultur-

The lively ceiling decoration, CENTER at the Toksu Palace, Seoul which probably dates back to the sixteenth century, depicts the dragon motive symbolizing authority and longevity.

ally and linguistically connected with the Finns, Mongols and Turks, who streamed down into the peninsula from northern and central Asia some 30,000 years ago. They constituted the most easterly outpost of Altaic culture. Thousands of years of interaction with the Japanese, whom they closely resemble physically, and the Chinese, to whom they are indebted for much of their culture, have complicated matters, but both in culture and language Korea remains a distinct and homogeneous entity. Take the language, for example. Along with the writing system, Korea borrowed a vast vocabulary from the Chinese, which remains the backbone of the nation's learning - yet the way of pronouncing these borrowed words is distinctly their own. Korean shares an identical sentence structure with Japanese, evidence of closely intertwined roots, yet the differences, too, are deep.

The Korean creation myth is curious and instructive. Hwanung, son of the divine creator, descended from heaven and proclaimed himself king of all he surveyed. While he was looking over his domain, he overheard the fervent prayers of a bear that desired to become human. Taking pity on the beast, Hwanung gave it twenty pieces of garlic and some mugwort, and told it to retire to a cave for a hundred days. The bear did as it was told. When it emerged, it was the first human woman.

This woman prayed for a son, became pregnant through divine favor, and shortly gave birth to one Tan-gun, who in 2333 BC became the first human king and the founder of Korea. His reign was of the epic length favored in those days - more than 1,200 years in fact, ending in 1122 BC. Tan-gun or National Foundation Day is still cele-

brated every year on October 3. (Most of Korea's public holidays are concentrated in the fall, by common consent the most agreeable season.)

The creation myth is interesting on account of the venerable age it accords to the nation's still quite striking attachment to garlic. It also suggests that herbal medicine goes back a long way into the nation's prehistory: mugwort remains an important ingredient in traditional cures.

At the end of Tan-gun's reign, the myth continues (now transmuting qui-

RIGHT Korea's largest standing stone Buddha, the Unjin Miruk at Nonsan, glimpsed through the windows of Kwanchok-sa Temple.

etly into legend), the primordial China connection was made: one King Kija arrived in the peninsula, a direct descendant of the Chinese Shang dynasty which collapsed that same year. 1122 BC thus saw the establishment of new dynasties in both China and Korea, and though the date is merely traditional, the story does attest to the ancient and largely fraternal links between Korea and its giant neighbor. China was the Central Kingdom, Korea was "Choson," the Land of Morning Calm. Korean kings, like Chinese emperors, took the dragon as their symbol of divine authority, but whereas the Chinese dragon had five claws, the Korean had only four - just to discourage people from entertaining foolish ideas.

The steady development of civilization in the peninsula during the first three millennia BC is evident in the wealth of archaeological remains. One of the oldest is the possibly Paleolithic dolmen still standing on the island of Kanghwa, near Seoul, which may date from the twentieth century BC. Sophisticated pottery remains from the first

millennia BC are not uncommon, then the elaborate articles produced by a Bronze Age culture which came down from Siberia via Manchuria begin to appear. This culture stimulated the appearance of tribal leagues, replacing the smaller clan organizations of the stone age, but was rapidly supplanted by iron-wielding groups which came down from northern China.

The first historically proven Chinese invasion of the peninsula came in 108 BC. After the Han Dynasty had put an end to dissent within China, the Han emperor Wu-ti invaded the ancient kingdom of Chosun and the regime he established retained control of the country for more than 400 years. Then in 313 AD the Koguryo tribe, based in the north of the country, which had been steadily growing in power for centuries, took advantage of the disintegration to wrest control of northern Korea and southeastern Manchuria from the Chinese. Though it adopted China's advanced military and administrative systems, Koguryo remained ethnically and culturally Korean.

THREE KINGDOMS: A CHINESE MIRROR

Meanwhile, further south on the Korean peninsula, two other powerful tribes emerged: the Paekche, which carved a kingdom out of the south-west corner, and the Shilla, which dominated the entire eastern portion of the peninsula. Like the three kingdoms who supplanted the Han dynasty in China, these three Korean kingdoms engaged in constant internecine warfare and political intrigue, and their relationship was marked by rapidly shifting alliances. Like the Three Kingdoms period in China, this was also in Korea an

era of great turbulence and intellectual ferment.

In 618, the house of T'ang defeated all other rivals for the Dragon Throne, and reunited the Chinese empire for the first time since the fall of Han. One of the T'ang dynasty's first objectives was to establish effective control over the Korean peninsula. In 645 and again in 647, T'ang armies attacked the Koguryo kingdom but failed to conquer it. So adopting the time-honored Chinese strategy of "using barbarians to subdue barbarians," the T'ang court formed an alliance with the southern Shilla kingdom, and together they defeated Paekche in 660 and 667. T'ang China next tried to vanquish Shilla as well.

Shilla, however, rebelled against T'ang hegemony, giving aid and encouragement to insurgents in Paekche and Koguryo, too. Under the Shilla banner the three men later eulogized as the unifiers of the nation, King Muyol, his successor King Munmu, and their military commander, General Kim, fought against heavy odds to drive the Chinese back across the Taedong River, north of the present North Korean capi-

ABOVE RIGHT Buddhist painting at Pomo-sa Temple near Pusan, headquarters of the Dyana sect.

tal, P'yongyang, and unify the entire Korean peninsula. In the process, Shilla also succeeded in establishing dominion over Paekche and Koguryo. An agreement was then drawn up which saved China's face on the one hand, and ensured Shilla's future security and independence on the other. According to this, Shilla would remain an independent Korean kingdom, but would also become an official tributary state of China, and acknowledge China's supremacy in the region. The art of diplomatic hair-splitting is by no means a new one.

THE PENINSULA UNITED

Historians generally agree that this unification of the peninsula in the seventh century by Shilla is the beginning of Korea's history as a united nation. Though this unity sometimes proved chimerical in subsequent centuries, it persisted more or less intact until the partitioning of the country in 1945.

The flow of Chinese cultural institutions into the peninsula, which had got seriously under way during the Three Kingdoms Period, continued after the triumph of Shilla. The Confucian principles of organizing society, which had evolved in China during the Han era, were gradually adopted in Korea as well, though with modifications. In particular the Korean ruling-class was unable to overcome its distaste for the egalitarianism intrinsic to the Chinese bureaucracy, whereby candidates of any and all social ranks could compete for positions in government. As in Japan, the form of the civil service examination was adopted, but in reality high office was reserved for the children of the aristocracy.

Under Chinese influence, the Three Kingdoms and Shilla Periods also saw the establishment of Buddhism throughout the peninsula, and a terrific flourishing of the associated arts and crafts, as well as the Chinese writing system.

During the United Shilla Dynasty that followed Shilla's military defeat of the Chinese, Korea began to exert strong influence on Japan, at this time emerging from the primitive twilight. As the closest point on the Asian continent to the Japanese archipelago, Korea was the route through which Chinese culture traveled to Japan, picking up a distinctive Korean flavor on the way. Korean scholars became tutors to the Japanese imperial house, and so many others traveled to Japan to serve in the administration that a family register made in 815 reveals that fully one-third of Japan's noble families were of Korean descent. This fact is ironic in the light of Japan's attempt earlier this century to stigmatize the Koreans as barbaric and to extinguish their language and culture in favor of Japan's.

As the T'ang dynasty in China began to crumble during the ninth century, so did the Shilla. Various branches of the royal clan plotted to seize power, peasants revolted and bandits ran amok

---

Musicians in annual Confucian ceremony at Chongmyo shrine, Seoul. The instrument is called a Pyonggyong; the chimes are made of a jade-like stone.

through the country. The Shilla dynasty began to fragment as petty kings set up petty tyrannies within its frontiers.

Then, just about the time that the house of Sung re-unified China, the Korean house of Koryo succeeded in doing the same thing for the peninsula. The dynasty they founded in 918 was to last for 450 years.

KORYO: A CULTURAL PEAK

The Koryo dynasty, from which the word Korea derives, was founded, not by an aristocrat but by the son of a merchant, Wang Kon by name. He was also the first ruler of the peninsula to invoke the Chinese concept of the "mandate of heaven," meaning that his claim to the throne was based on moral rather than hereditary grounds.

The dominant cultural role during the Koryo dynasty was played by Buddhism, which was generously patronized by the Koryo kings and became a powerful force in politics. Numerous temples and pagodas were built, and Buddhist statuary attained new peaks of artistic excellence. In fact, the early years of Koryo were a flourishing time for Korean culture in general. Celadon porcelain was mastered by the nation's potters, who went on to make works unsurpassed even by the Chinese. The principle of movable type was invented by a Korean, and books were printed with it, two hundred years before Gutenberg started doing the same thing in Europe. Intellectually the most important event was the introduction from China of the ideas of Neo-Confucianism, which brought about the first organized intellectual opposition to Buddhism.

Like the Sung dynasty in China, Koryo was plagued by political pressures from the north. The northern Khitan tribe, after sacking the Sung capital and sending the court into exile, attempted in 993 to invade Koryo, but was successfully repelled. The next

challenge, however, demolished everything in its path: the Mongol alliance, led by Genghis Khan, which destroyed all rivals on the northern steppes and then began its relentless campaign to conquer China and the rest of the known world.

In 1231 Ghengis Khan's troops attacked Korea in full force, but met with unexpectedly stiff resistance. Meanwhile the Koryo court retreated into exile on Kanghwa Island (taking advantage of the Mongols' one weakness, fear of the sea), and there the king ordered the engraving on 80,000 wooden tablets of the *Tripitaka Koreana*, based on the complete Chinese translation of the Buddhist Scripture. Once it was completed the entire work was committed to the flames - an offering to the gods to enlist their protection against the Mongols. (Another complete set of the Scriptures was later carved, and is preserved at the famous Haein Temple, near Taegu. (See **Korea: The Broad Highway**, page 73)

LIVING WITH THE MONGOLS

Their prayers were only partially answered. When the Mongols set up their Yuan dynasty in China, Koryo was

Embroidered decoration on the costume of officiating Confucian priest at Chongmyo shrine, central Seoul. OPPOSITE Archaic front view of Confucian scholar at Chongmyo.

obliged to come to terms with them. The country was allowed a show of independence and continued to rule most of the peninsula, but in reality it was a tributary state of the Yuan. And the Koryo was forced to accept many distasteful conditions: the crown princes were obliged to go to the new Chinese capital, Peking, for their education, to marry Mongol princesses, and to remain there as hostages until the reigning Koryo king died. By this means the Mongols gained effective control of the country, without having to go to the trouble of conquering it. They also extorted a heavy annual tribute in the form of gold, silver, ginseng and women.

When Chinese rebels under the leadership of the peasant general Chu Yuan-chang routed the Mongols and drove them back across the Great Wall, Korea gained a brief reprieve. The hundred-year-long humiliation was over. But within twenty years of the establishment of the Ming dynasty in 1386, the Chinese were once again trying to gain control of Korea. An invading army was dispatched to the country, and the Koryo court responded by sending a fiery young commander named Yi Song-gye to repel the invaders.

Yi realized, however, that his army stood no chance of success against the superior Ming force, so he turned back and promptly deposed the Koryo king, at first replacing him with the crown prince but later taking the throne himself. In 1392, invoking the mandate of heaven, Yi established the Yi dynasty, also known as the Choson dynasty, Choson being the ancient Chinese name for Korea. It was to become both Korea's last and its longest dynasty, surviving until the Japanese annexation in 1910. Yi, who was given the title T'aejo or Founding Father of the new dynasty, immediately re-established traditional tributary relations with China, adopted Neo-Confucianism as the

new state creed, and re-named his kingdom Choson, in the Chinese style. He moved the capital of the nation to Hanyang, the city known today as Seoul.

YI: THE LONGEST ERA

The adoption of Neo-Confucianism, which had first reared its head during the Koryo period, was highly significant for Korean society. For one thing, it mollified the conservative Ming court, which commenced to regard Korea once again as a dutiful younger brother, capable of managing its own affairs. For another, it greatly reduced the influence of Buddhism, both at court and in the daily life of the people. Confucian burial rites, for instance, took the place of Buddhist cremation, and ancestor-worship and other Confucian practices became *de rigueur*.

King Sejong, the fourth Yi ruler, who reigned from 1418 to 1450, is gen-

HIDEYOSHI'S HUBRIS

Though the Japanese triumphed easily on land, at sea it was a different matter. The commander of the Korean fleet, Admiral Yi Sun-shin gave his navy an unexpected advantage with his invention of the world's first armor-plated warships, called Turtle Ships on account of their humped appearance. Propelled by oars and heavily armed with cannon, these compact, highly-maneuverable vessels had decks and gunwales plated with spike-studded sheets of heavy iron, making them impossible to board and practically invulnerable to enemy projectiles. Though greatly outnumbered by the Japanese, Admiral Yi's handful of Turtle Ships sent the Japanese into a panic, sinking more than 250 ships in the course of eight battles and forcing the Japanese to withdraw before they had succeeded even in setting foot on Chinese soil.

Provoked by Korea's stubborn resistance, Hideyoshi launched another attack in 1597. Admiral Yi, meanwhile, had fallen victim to Korean court intrigues and had lost his post. His successor sallied forth to meet the second Japanese onslaught - and promptly lost all but a dozen of the Korean fleet. Yi was hastily recalled, and with only this handful of ships at his disposal once again routed the numerically superior Japanese, sinking or capturing most of their ships and putting the rest to flight. During the final battle of the war, Yi was struck by a stray bullet and killed. He continues to live on in the popular imagination as Korea's greatest military leader, and his armored statue still glares down from its pedestal in central Seoul.

erally regarded as Korea's greatest king. He filled the highest offices with men of merit, and under his influence the nation's culture flourished as never before. It was King Sejong who personally supervised the creation of *han'gul*, the unique Korean alphabet which freed Korean literature and education from its cumbersome dependence on complex ideograms.

Once again, however, the nation's hard-earned calm was soon rudely shattered by outside events. This time the intrusion came from Japan, when the shogun Hideyoshi launched his megalomanic campaign to conquer China in 1592. The Yi court declined to participate, and in retribution Hideyoshi attacked Korea with a force of 150,000 men. The Japanese army swept through the peninsula, overwhelming Korea's land defenses in less than a month and wreaking such havoc wherever they went that the Koreans have never forgotten nor forgiven it.

ABOVE Relic of Shilla dynasty Buddhist image in stone, preserved at the National Museum, Kyongju.

Hideyoshi's death in 1598 persuaded the Japanese to abandon their continental adventure, but the ensuing peace was once again short-lived. The Manchus came next, when their leader Nurhachi initiated his own campaign to conquer Ming China. In 1627, Manchu cavalry swept down from the north and captured both P'yongyang and Seoul, forcing the Yi court to break off its long-standing tributary relationship with China and become a Manchu vassal instead.

In 1636, Korea rebelled against the Manchu overlords, and in response the Manchus once again crossed the Yalu River in force, this time capturing the entire court and exacting heavy revenge. Eight years later, in 1644, they decisively defeated the Ming in China, occupied Peking, and established China's last dynasty, the Ching. Korea became a tributary state of Ching, and remained so until Japan wrested control away from China at the turn of the present century. Interestingly, the last dynasties of both China and Korea were to fall within a year of each other.

LICKING THE WOUNDS

After the consecutive traumas of the Japanese and Manchu invasions, which left the whole country in ruins and the people instilled with a fear of all foreigners, Korea pulled back into its shell and enforced a policy of thoroughgoing isolation. It became the Hermit Kingdom, insular and aloof - and, in consequence, lamentably ill-equipped to meet the challenges of a new age when, in the nineteenth century, the European and Japanese imperialists came knocking loudly on the door. Korea strove manfully to keep them all out, but with the Ching dynasty in Peking, its ostensible protector, in a state of terminal decline, collapse was only a matter of time.

From the middle of the nineteenth century the Hermit Kingdom had been proving less than hermetic, and Western learning had begun to filter into the country by way of Peking. Much of this came via Catholic missionaries, who naturally tried to spread their faith at the same time. The Yi court, however, regarded Catholicism as a serious threat to Korea's traditional Confucian order and tried to suppress it. The court issued repeated warnings and edicts against the Christian faith and severely punished offenders. In 1866, nine French Catholic priests were publicly executed on the banks of the Han River in Seoul, and 8,000 Korean converts were massacred in the pogroms that followed.

The Chinese were the only foreigners freely admitted into Korea during these years. European and American diplomats and merchants were excluded rigorously, and this policy was extended to include the Japanese when it was felt that they had been tainted by Western influence. The Japanese took offense at this, and in 1875 deliberately provoked an incident between ships of their navy and Korean coastal defenses. Taking its cue from Western "gunboat diplomacy," Japan used the ensuing peace negotiations to force Korea to permit Japanese diplomatic and trade missions to be established on Korean soil.

Japanese influence on the peninsula grew rapidly in the wake of that treaty, much to the dismay of the Korean government, which was still nominally a tributary of China. Chinese troops were sent from Peking to re-assert Ching authority, and clashed repeatedly on Korean soil with Japanese forces.

Years of aggressive foreign pressure, Japanese, Chinese and Western, provoked a patriotic and xenophobic reaction which found expression in the

RIGHT The Un Dang *Yogwan* in Seoul, formally the house of a nobleman, and one of the few which offer a rich experience of the traditional way of Korean life.

Tonghak ("Eastern Learning") Movement, a grassroots social and religious movement which proposed applying traditional Eastern learning to the task of keeping out the foreigners and saving the country from ruin. These efforts culminated in the Tonghak Uprising of 1894, which in turn sparked off the Sino-Japanese War. A small peasant uprising in Cholla Province led quickly to major rebel victories over government forces, causing the government to petition China for assistance. China sent an army across the Yalu to help the Korean government to suppress the revolt, at which Japan responded by sending an army of its own into the peninsula.

JAPAN'S LITTLE EMPIRE

Within a year Japan had dealt the decadent Ching court a comprehensive and humiliating defeat, and forced it to accept the terms of the Treaty of Shimonoseki, which formally ended hostilities on April 17, 1895. This treaty guaranteed Korea's independence from China - a doubtful blessing, for in Chi-

na's place the treaty gave Japan a key role in Korean affairs, a role which led to outright annexation fifteen years later. Japan also demanded and got control of both the Ryukyu Islands (Okinawa) and Taiwan, and formally annexed both the same year.

The next uninvited guest at the banquet Korea was haplessly making of itself for the modernized nations was Russia, which competed fiercely with Japan for influence at the Korean court. The eventual consequence of this was the Russo-Japanese War of 1904, when the Japanese once again showed the mettle of their new armed forces by obtaining a clear victory. In the aftermath Japan immediately occupied Korea, and in the Treaty of Portsmouth, which ended hostilities on September 5, 1905, Japan's control over Korea was given international recognition. It was a small step from this to the rendering of Korea into Japan's very own Western-style colony. Japan's resident-general became the ultimate authority in Korea, wielding total control over the country's foreign relations, internal administration and police force.

Korean patriots offered stiff resistance to the Japanese, and formed guerrilla bands to harass them. In 1909 the Japanese resident-general, Ito Hirobumi, was assassinated by a Korean patriot while visiting Harbin in Manchuria, and in retaliation Japan dictated a new treaty the following year, under which Korea was annexed entirely and Korean statehood abolished.

From then on, the Japanese ruled Korea with an iron fist, ruthlessly suppressing any sign of opposition. The greatest threat to their authority came in 1919 when Korean nationalists, in common with other victims of colonialism in many other nations, submitted a petition to the Versailles Conference demanding independence. When their demand was rejected they unilaterally published a "declaration of independence," demanding the immediate withdrawal of Japanese forces. As the movement gathered momentum, and peaceful demonstrations began to occur spontaneously throughout the country, the Japanese police panicked, and attacked the patriots for week after week with brutally excessive force, leaving thousands of unarmed civilians dead. The few concessions they subsequently made to Korean pride did nothing to weaken their grip on the country, but in the longer perspective the independence movement had some positive consequences for Korea. It gave the lie to the Japanese myth that their control of Korea was benign and had the support of the mass of the people; and it did much to develop a sense of national solidarity among Koreans.

KOREA'S DARK VALLEY

As the militarists in the Japanese government gained the upper hand during the 1930s, repression in Korea once again increased, and a cruel campaign was launched to eradicate Korean culture and replace it with Japanese models. Ancient palaces and temples were razed or bulldozed, masters of Korean arts were killed or interned to prevent

OPPOSITE PAGE Baggy traditional garments and wonderful hats are still often seen in rural areas of Korea; but ABOVE city children are as gaudy and individualistic in their choice of clothes as Americans.

THE BRIEF PEACE

With the defeat of the Japanese in 1945, Korea enjoyed yet another of its pathetically brief interludes of peace. Two new occupying forces now swarmed across the country, the Russian and the American, disarming the Japanese, and while the arbitrarily selected 38th parallel was initially intended merely as a demarcation line for the efforts of these allied forces, it soon hardened into an unbreachable boundary between powers which proved to have very different plans for Korea's future. The Russians went straight to work establishing a fully-fledged Communist regime in the north, with Kim Il-Sung as its ruler, while the Americans withdrew from the south, which quickly fell into political disarray.

In September 1947, the United Nations called for the establishment of a united and independent Korean state, and suggested that national elections be held to determine its government. The Soviet Union, however, refused to permit the UN to supervise elections in the north, and so they were held only in the south. On August 15, 1948 the Republic of Korea came officially into being, with Syngman Rhee as its democratically elected (and very right-wing) president and Seoul as its capital. The Soviet-controlled north reacted by establishing the "Democratic Republic of Korea" on September 9 of the same year, with Kim Il-sung as head of state and P'yongyang as its capital. For the first time since the uniting of the Three Kingdoms under the Shilla dynasty in the seventh century, Korea found itself divided into politically antagonistic entities.

By the end of 1948, Russian and American troops had withdrawn from their opposite ends of the peninsula, but

them from spreading Korean culture to a new generation. Korean history was summarily dropped from school curricula, and all courses were subsequently taught entirely in Japanese. Koreans were forced to adopt Japanese names, the Japanese language and Japanese manners. Thousands of Korean men were pressed into Japan's armed forces or shipped to Japan as slave labor for the war effort, while Korean women were rounded up to perform as prostitutes for Japan's occupation troops.

Japanese colonial rule in Korea brought significant material improvements in terms of new schools, hospitals, roads, railways and communication systems, and stimulated the modernization of industry and agriculture. But as in colonies everywhere, the country's development was oriented to the needs of the colonial power, and the country's labor and resources were relentlessly exploited for the benefit of Japan. Awareness of the richness of Korea's national heritage has been slow to re-awaken; bitterness at the rapacity of Japanese power has been equally slow to dissipate.

ABOVE Setting sun over Seoul. RIGHT In Seoul's Namsan Park, forsythia and cherry blossom leave city dwellers in no doubt that spring has sprung.

while the United States did little to enhance the south's defenses, the Russians continued to pour arms and advisers into the north, building up a formidable North Korean army. Then in January 1950, the American. Secretary of State declared in public that Korea lay beyond the pale of America's vital interests. The North Koreans, confident of their superiority in arms, were not slow to take the hint and on June 25, 1950 launched a full-scale invasion of the south.

With the Soviet delegate to the United Nations conveniently not in attendance, the United States managed to get a UN resolution passed branding the North Koreans as aggressors, and pledging UN troops in the south's defense. Although the great majority of the troops sent to resist the north were American, the forces of fifteen other nations fought North Korea under the United Nations flag.

At first the invaders from the north routed the UN troops, and nearly succeeded in driving them clean off the peninsula: the southern port city of Pusan was the only center of population they did not reach. But then General Douglas MacArthur, the American commander, conceived and executed a daring amphibious landing at Inch'on, west of Seoul, cutting off over-extended North Korean forces and turning the tide of the war. Despite strong warnings from China not to do so, MacArthur pursued the enemy across the 38th Parallel deep into the north.

As United States forces approached the Manchurian border, Chinese troops suddenly began pouring across the Yalu River, drove the UN side back across the 38th Parallel again and recaptured Seoul. For the first time in history Chinese and American soldiers confronted each other on the battlefield, but for Korea the scene was all-too familiar. "When whales fight, the shrimp gets hurt" says a Korean proverb, and the Korean War hurt the country more than any previous conflict. Bloody battles raged back and forth across the peninsula, with heavy casualties and massive destruction on both sides.

EYEBALL TO EYEBALL

Finally, on July 27, 1953, an armistice ended the fighting and formally divided Korea at the 38th Parallel, with a three-mile wide Demilitarized Zone (DMZ) in between. This belt of no-man's-land is supervised by a joint north/south Military Armistice Commission, which has been meeting regularly at P'anmunjom since 1953 to discuss alleged truce violations and exchange accusations. They are the longest continuing truce talks in the history of human cussedness.

At the end of the Korean War, Syngman Rhee presided over a nation laid waste by modern warfare and a government staffed entirely by his personal protégés. Seoul and most of the countryside were in ruins, industry and agriculture had ground to a halt, and corruption was rampant at every level of government. As conditions grew steadily worse during the 1950s, popular resentment against the Rhee regime began to gather momentum.

Elections were held again in 1960, but they were so obviously rigged in Rhee's favor that anti-government demonstrations flared up all over the country. The culminating event came in Seoul, when police fired on angry crowds and killed 115 people. Under heavy pressure from all sides, Rhee wisely resigned from office and retired to Hawaii, where he died in 1965.

On August 15, 1960 South Korea's Second Republic was established under the leadership of Rhee's former opponents in the Democratic Party. The new

RIGHT United Nations soldier standing guard at P'anmunjom, the only place where the Koreas meet. The height and other dimensions of the two flags have been the subject of endless exercises in one-upmanship.

government was refreshingly open and liberal, but soon proved to be hopelessly ineffectual in dealing with the country's pressing problems, and was toppled by a military coup in May 1961. A military dictatorship with a strong anti-communist stance took over, and before long Major-General Park Chung Hee emerged as its leader. Park called for new elections in 1963, retired from the military, and ran successfully for president. He was inaugurated in December, and Korea's Third Republic was launched.

IN PARK'S POCKET

Park won a second presidential term in 1967, and then in 1969 he forced through a constitutional amendment which permitted him to run yet again. In 1971 he narrowly defeated opposition leader Kim Dae-jung for a third presidential term, and the following year tightened his stranglehold on Korean affairs by declaring martial law. He took all effective political power into his own hands, and ruled by decree.

Despite the arbitrary nature of his regime, Korea did attain a degree of stability under Park, and the economy took great strides. His government threw its full support behind industrial growth, with special emphasis on exports, and during the 1960s the economy achieved a spectacular annual growth rate of over forty per cent. Even during the 1970s, as other countries struggled to cope with the oil crisis, Korea maintained a steady export growth of about fifteen per cent per year. By 1979 the total value of Korea's exports had topped US$14 billion.

The nation's economic development was well-planned from the outset. Heavy industries were distributed through the country, not concentrated in and around the capital. Modern expressways were built which gave rapid access to the new centers of industry both from Seoul and from the international seaports of Pusan and Inch'on.

Initially the great bulk of assistance went to heavy industry, but a serious attempt was made to right this with the creation in 1970 of the Saemaul (New Community) Movement, which aimed to modernize agriculture and rural life in general through spurring villagers to help themselves. The results are seen everywhere one travels in the countryside: neat villages of modern brick houses, usually with a metal church spire somewhere in their midst; neatly-tilled fields, blinding with vinyl sleeves; and innumerable small tractors and harvesters at work (though you will also be delighted to spot the occasional farmer plowing his patch with the help of an ox, or trundling into market behind a bullock.)

The Park era came abruptly to an end on October 26, 1979, when the president was assassinated at a banquet by the hand-picked chief of his own security organization, the Korean CIA. The assassin claimed that his motive was simply to end Park's dictatorial hold over the country and restore democracy, but the court gave him little sympathy, and he and six accomplices were convicted and executed. After eighteen years under Park's rule, the Republic of Korea suddenly found itself in a frightening political vacuum.

The answer, after a brief hiatus when Park's prime minister held the reins, was another strong man from the army. In August 1980 General Chun Doo Hwan took charge, and the next month was formally inaugurated as president. He remains in charge today, though he is pledged to relinquish control by 1988, when presidential elections are due to be held.

PROSPERITY AND PROTEST

Under Chun, the nation's economy has continued to prosper but steps towards democracy have so far been tentative at best. Kim Dae-jung, President Park's old *bête noir*, returned from exile in the United States, but both he and the other most prominent opposition politician, Kim Young-sam, found their potential for action closely restricted by Chun. Eager to present the world with a clean, respectable, democratic face, yet lacking a popular base of his own and terrified of the advantage North Korea might take of any sign of weakness,

Chun walks a difficult path.

Despite the fantastic economic achievements, which have put the Republic in a different league from the north and have done much to narrow the gap between rich and poor and city- and country-dwellers, its way forward is by no means clear. Democracy is keenly desired, as the passionate anti-Chun demonstrations on Seoul's campuses each spring make clear. But the nation's experience of democracy is almost nil, and attempts in the near-future to make it work will doubtless have to

put up with having the military hovering nervously in the background, ready to intervene at any moment. When the basic question of how the country should be governed is fraught with such difficulties, it is not surprising that the larger issue of how the peninsula might be united is even tougher to resolve. But that improbable event is surely the desideratum at the back of most Koreans' minds. Until it comes to pass, even massive prosperity will not succeed in cloaking the fact that, on either side of the DMZ, what is being lived is only half a life.

Symbols, OPPOSITE, of State and ABOVE of growing industrial sophistication.

A trait of epic stubbornness has enabled Korea to hang on to the particulars of its culture through thick and thin; the little hiccup which goes by the name of modernization has so far failed miserably to turn the country into a clone of New Jersey, Birmingham or Osaka, however much it may in superficial ways have come to resemble them. Growing prosperity has indeed in one sense had the opposite effect: it has permitted evidence of the wealth of their tradition, many Koreans who lived through the period of Japanese domination experience deep emotion. Gazing at the amazingly beautiful and serene stone Buddha in Sokkuram grotto, near Kyongju, one guide remarked, "Every time I come here I feel I've found something that we lost a long, long time ago."

For the visitor, Korea's rich mix of cultural elements, most of which are in varying degrees unfamiliar, can be baffling. In the space of a few weeks' stay in Seoul he might witness ancient rites

money and effort to go into rediscovering or even re-creating what has been lost. Potters now travel to Japan to study the techniques that disappeared from the peninsula when Hideyoshi's invaders prevailed on the country's best artisans to go back to Japan with them. Immense care is taken to preserve and display the archaeological relics dug up in places like Kyongju, capital during the Shilla period, and to restore extant historical sites to their original condition. Confronted by this of Confucianism, Buddhism and Shamanism, as well as attending a crowded Catholic mass and a superb recital of classical European music. He is entitled to know how it all fits together, and what sort of sense it makes.

RELIGION

SHAMAN ROOTS

When disaster befalls a Korean household - if one of the members falls seriously ill, or if the house is repeatedly burgled, or if the husband seems bent on tearing the family apart by spending all his money on his mistress - a traditional Korean housewife knows that there is only one thing to be done: call in a reputable *mudang* and conduct a *kut*.

The *mudang* is a shamanistic medium, and the *kut* is the elaborate ceremony, lasting long hours and sometimes all night, through which, to the accompaniment of cacophonous music, the *mudang* communicates with the spirits infesting the house, driving out the evil ones and placating the benevolent ones with offerings of food, drink and money. The closest analogy in the West is the exorcism rite, and as in an exorcism the *mudang's* role involves her being taken over by several spirits turn while she is in a trance. Her behavior in this state may be wild and unpredictable, and invariably leaves her exhausted.

Belief in the spirit world and in the

necessity of interceding with it is found all over the world, from Haiti to the suburbs of South-east England, but perhaps nowhere else has it retained so strong a hold on the popular imagination over such a long period of time.

Shamanism is the basic bedrock of Korean culture. The word shaman, which entered English through German, is Siberian in origin, and the tissue of beliefs and practices with which it is associated probably entered the peninsula with the Altaic settlers from the north, deep in the prehistoric past. Quite early it made the jump to Japan, where it slowly mutated into what is known as the "indigenous" religion, Shinto.

Like Shinto, Korean shamanism benefited from the tolerant attitude of Buddhism, which had become the state religion of the whole peninsula by the sixth century, Shilla being the last kingdom to succumb to it. Suppression of practices inimical to Buddhism, such as human sacrifice, occurred gradually during the following centuries, but there was no systematic attempt to outlaw shamanism. It has retained a great deal of popular loyalty right up to the present.

Confucianism, more a civil code than a religion, was unsympathetic to shamanism but failed to uproot it. In fact, according to one theory, it unintentionally gave shamanism an extra lease of life. In the pre-Confucian days, *mudang* came in both sexes. When the male-chauvinistic code of Confucianism became established, Korean women found themselves at the bottom of the heap. Not only had they lost hope of attaining high status in society, but even the basic human pleasures, sexual pleasure included, were denied them and regarded as insignificant. The result, it is suggested, was a terrific incidence of

OPPOSITE Some of the thousands of woodblocks inscribed with Buddhist texts which have resided for more than 700 years at the Haein-sa Temple. LEFT Gilt statue of a Bodhisattva from the United Shilla Kingdom (668-935).

lems of modern Korean life. He could hardly be more wrong.

Confucianism is everywhere in Korea today, scarcely less vigorous and ubiquitous than in the past. The young male foreigner may get his first taste of it at the airport, when the Immigration Officer tells him frankly that he is too young to wear a beard, which is the prerogative of the aged. But that's only the start of it.

If he inquires among the honeymoon couples thronging Cheju-do island, he will discover that all the brides are two,

three or four years younger than their spouses, and that many of the marriages were arranged. Chatting with a young Korean friend at the latter's home he will be surprised at the way his friend extinguishes his cigarette as soon as his father enters the room. The father points out with pride what a good, respectful son he has, for smoking in front of elders is not done. On that Sunday in May at Chongmyo Shrine, after the ceremony, an old man in traditional costume and a long white beard standing near the entrance conducts an apparently hilarious monologue while his

middle-aged listeners nod approvingly and youngsters hang on every word. What is he talking about? The Confucian virtues (particularly filial piety), and why they must be kept up.

Confucianism is the moral backbone of Korea, and while the rebellious young may kick against its rigid rules, anyone who remarks approvingly on the honesty, the courtesy, the dignity and the considerateness of Koreans is to a great extent admiring the effects of Confucianism. In China the same code has long been diluted due to that country's greater social mobility and ethnic diversity. In Japan, Confucian behavior persists but its origins are rarely mentioned. Only among Koreans, "the ceremonious people of the East" as the Chinese used to describe them, does it retain its old power, skillfully reinforced by military and industrial hierarchies which find it a matchless way of keeping the game under control.

When Confucianism arrived in the tenth century, it found rich soil in Korea's homogeneous and hierarchical society. Four centuries later, in 1392, Yi Song-gye established the Yi dynasty, and one of his most important reforms was to give official approval to the new, stricter variation of Confucian social ethics and the conservative worldview known now as Neo-Confucianism. Neo-Confucianism froze the social order, made filial piety the ultimate social virtue and required that ancestor worship be the most important religious ceremony in every household. It stressed the supreme importance of harmony and propriety in social relationships, each of which was now governed by specific rules of decorum, or *li*.

The main victims of this ascendancy of Neo-Confucianism were Korean women, and they are still suffering today. In the past, while a new baby boy was lovingly admired on a bed, baby girls were placed on the floor. Girls received no formal education;

ABOVE Bells used during a Confucian ceremony in Seoul. RIGHT Portrait of one of the most eminent of Yi dynasty Confucian scholars, Yi Chae.

missionaries began to stream into the country, Presbyterians and Methodists being the most successful in attracting followers. At the beginning of the present century Korea was widely regarded as one of the best places in the world for missionary endeavor.

A major reason for the missionaries' success was that they brought all sorts of Western learning with them besides Christianity, and thus attracted many of the most intelligent and energetic into their flocks. They also established the first schools and colleges for women, and when the country was annexed by Japan, missionaries strongly supported the independence effort, which further endeared them to the people at large. The Japanese ended up expelling them en masse in 1940.

Korean Christianity has its own flavor. Many Protestant congregations have a strong evangelical streak, while many Catholic converts show strong tendencies to mysticism - perhaps a reflection of the country's long tradition of shamanism.

Today there are more than eight million Christians in Korea, of whom

some eighty per cent are Protestant. While Christians account for only about twenty per cent of the population, they include many leaders of the intellectual

Early bastions of Christianity in Seoul, TOP the Anglican Cathedral in Chong Dong, the city's original foreign quarter; ABOVE the interior of St Mary's Cathedral in Myong Dong. RIGHT Nuns enjoying the Seoul spring.

too, for the old days when the sexes had separate and almost inviolable territory have gone for good.

The paper used with such versatility in the Korean home has a long history. Introduced from China about a thousand years ago, its manufacture was perfected in Korea, and even today hand-made Korean paper is prized by Chinese and Japanese calligraphers for its durability and special absorbent qualities. Paper for windows, screens and *ondol* floors, as well as for painting and calligraphy, is still made by hand in the city of Chonju.

CERAMICS: "ONE OF THE WONDERFUL THINGS"

Ceramics is another area of traditional Korean excellence. Most famous of all, and much imitated by Korean potters today, is the celadon porcelain produced during the Koryo Period. "Celadon" refers to an iron-bearing glaze used by the craftsmen of that period to produce pottery of uncannily beautiful blue-green shades. Although the celadon technique was Chinese in origin, Korean craftsmen produced colors of a peculiar subtlety which the Chinese admired greatly but proved unable to reproduce. A Chinese scholar of the Sung period declared that this mysterious color was one of the ten most wonderful things in the world - the other nine all being Chinese.

The dictionary says celadon means "willow-green," but expert eyes can distinguish over sixty different shades of this subtle color, from a very light yellowish green to an almost brown hue. The most prized shades are "kingfisher-blue," "sky blue after rain," and "sea water washed by rain and wind." By the mid-twelfth century, Koreans had developed their own unique inlay method, whereby designs were inscribed into the wet clay, then the entire piece smeared with soft white clay. When the excess white clay was wiped away from the surface, the inlaid designs remained filled with white. The piece was then glazed with celadon and fired.

Not only the colors but the frank,

LEFT Five-story pagoda of temple in Songni-san National Park. ABOVE Some of the dozens of structures of Pulguk-sa Temple, near Kyongju.

Korean music and dance differ significantly from the Western tradition. For one thing, in Korea the two almost always go together. For another, there are no strict rules of choreography and no rigorous formal techniques which must be perfected and repeated exactly at every performance. Spontaneity and improvisation rather than strict adherence to set forms are the crucial points in both music and dance. Instead of telling a story, Korean dance strives to evoke moods and convey feelings. The two key concepts are *hung* (the inner feeling or mood) and *mut* (charm, grace, spiritual inspiration), and their realization depend on the performer's inner resources rather than technique pure and simple.

In Korean dance, arm and upper torso movements are of central importance, while the feet generally remain concealed beneath billowing floor-length robes. Fluid, curving, continuous motions are emphasized, and dancers rarely pause to strike poses. The flowing costumes further enhance the fluidity of Korean dance, and performers often appear to float rather than step across the stage.

Korean dance takes three major forms, court, religious and folk. Traditional court dances were performed by male dancers as well as royal *kisaeng* for the entertainment of the royal family and their retinue - commoners never had a chance to see them. There were two distinct types, *hyang-ak* (of Korean origin) and *t'ang-ak* (of Chinese origin). While the steps were relatively simple, the costumes were highly elaborate. The most popular form was *Hwanganmu,* the "flower crown dance," so named for the small sparkling crown worn by the performers.

Religious dances also came in three distinct types: shaman, Buddhist and Confucian. Shaman dances, usually performed by

RIGHT Eclectically decorated fan, used in Shamanistic ceremony on the east coast; ABOVE Dyana Sect painting from Pomosa Temple, near Pusan.

female *mudang*, were central to the *kut*, and were used both to invoke the spirits and to launch the *mudang* into a trance. Buddhist dances were used to entreat Buddhist deities to smooth the way for departed souls on their journey to heaven. Confucian dances were highly ceremonious forms originally derived from China. They are distinguished, as one might expect, by stiff movements and rigid adherence to form. They still can be seen twice a year in spring and autumn, at Sungkyungkwan University, and once a year, on the first Sunday in May, at the Confucian Ceremonies held at Chongmyo Royal Shrine in Seoul.

The most quintessential Korean dances are the folk forms, which retain strong shamanistic overtones. It is in these dances that the idea of expressing inner emotions through outward gestures is most apparent. The oldest and most popular folk dance is the Farmer's Dance, in which the performers spin madly about the stage or floor to the urgent rhythms of drums and gongs. The Farmer's Dance is still performed as a shamanistic rite to purify dwellings, entreat the kindness of benevolent spirits, and exorcise evil forces.

Korea's most distinctive folk dance is the mask-dance drama, which usually satirizes the human frailty of monks and aristocrats. The vividly painted masks are expressive and grotesque. Made of wood, gourd or papier-mâché, they were traditionally burned after each performance in the belief that after use they became contaminated by spirits. Some survived, however, and still serve as models for contemporary mask-makers.

The mask-dance drama served as a folk outlet for the expression of popular resentment against a corrupt clergy and a grasping and oppressive ruling-class. Lechery was the most popular theme, and obscene remarks flew back and forth during the performances. Flutes, cymbals and drums provided the accompaniment. *Bongsan* is the title of the most popular of these dance-dramas.

Among Korea's folk dances, the most powerfully expressive are the solo forms known as *sungmu* and *salpuri*. The *sungmu*, or Buddhist Priest Dance, enacts the seduction of a monk renowned for his chastity by a *kisaeng*, Hwang Chin-I, who was famous for her talent at this sort of thing. Swaying before the monk's cave while beating a beguiling rhythm on her drum, the *kisaeng* brought the show to a climax

51

herbal medicine were already ancient arts in China and Korea at the dawn of written history. Prior to that, herbal medicine was the domain of shamans, who experimented with the medicinal properties of plants, minerals and animal products and passed this hard-earned knowledge on to their successors. The Chinese characters for "medicine" and "doctor" first appeared some three thousand years ago, marking the transition from shaman healers to professional physicians and pharmacists.

The principles of Chinese medicine were introduced into the court of Koguryo in the year 561. This knowledge quickly spread to the neighboring Paekche and Shilla kingdoms, where it blended with native Korean folk wisdom to create a hybrid medical art. Traditional Korean medicine, *hanyak*, was born from this marriage.

Hanyak continued to develop rapidly during the Koryo dynasty, and during the Yi era, an age of scholarship, Korean medical manuals and pharmacopoeias began to appear in great profusion. Over the centuries much of this Chinese and Korean medical knowledge filtered into Japan, where it formed the basis for traditional medicine there.

Korean medicine reached its zenith in 1610 with the publication of a massive 25-volume Korean pharmacopoeia called *Tong-I Pogam* (Treasures of Eastern Medicine). Compiled and written over a period of sixteen years by the court physician Ho Jun, this comprehensive and remarkably accurate medical manual is still used today by herbal doctors and pharmacists throughout the Orient.

Despite fierce competition from *yak-guk* (Western medicine), *hanyak* continues to thrive throughout Korea. Herbal shops in Seoul and elsewhere still stock everything from chrysanthemum petals for headaches and rhemannia root for heart ailments, to snake wine for impotence and dried tortoise for lumbago. Acupressure massage, acupuncture, moxibustion, pulse diagnosis, herbal diets, calisthenics, deep-breathing and other aspects of the great East Asian medical tradition also continue to flourish in modern Korea, primarily because Western medicine has proved incapable of coping with many of man's most troublesome ailments.

The difference between Western and traditional Eastern attitudes to the medical profession is instructive. In ancient Korea, families used to retain a doctor to supervise the health of its members, much as modern American corporations retain attorneys. The doctor would visit the family regularly, dispensing herbal prescriptions and medical advice and watching for signs of weakness or disease in each patient's health. Should a member of the family fall seriously ill, the doctor was held responsible for not preventing it, and all payment to him ceased. The doctor was then obliged to cure the patient - at his own expense! Only when he succeeded did payments resume. If he failed he lost an entire family of patients, as well as a lot of face. Under such a system it is hardly surprising that preventive medicine made great strides.

Prevention is at the heart of Korean and Chinese medicine. A patient's overall condition is analyzed in the the light of such diverse factors as the functional inter-relationships between his organs, his emotional life, his immediate physical environment, his diet, his sexual habits, the weather, the season and the local geography. Once the doctor has studied all these factors to obtain a complete picture of the patient's condition, he then prescribes herbal supplements, offers dietary advice and applies a variety of therapeutic methods to compensate for deficiencies, suppress

dried jujubes (so-called "Chinese dates") and pine nuts, boiled together with a little sugar. Drunk as a tonic stimulant, this potion increases potency and physical strength, improves the circulation and promotes an efficient metabolism. Ginger tea (*saeng kang cha*) is brewed from ginger root and raw sugar, and is highly recommended for fighting chills and preventing colds in winter. Various other health-giving concoctions are available. All are made by boiling the herbal ingredients in water with a little raw sugar until the liquid is reduced by about one-third.

Ginseng is strictly controlled a government monopoly bureau, which oversees every aspect of production and marketing. Quality control is rigorous, and prices are uniform throughout the country. It is sold everywhere in Korea and remains one of the country's best bargains, regardless of its price, for ginseng is a long-term investment in good health.

KOREAN CUISINE

A LUSTY ART

If it's true that you are what you eat, then the vibrant, dynamic nature of the Korean people might well be traced to their diet. The least known of the culinary traditions of Asia, Korean cuisine is the best evidence there is of the nation's cultural distinctiveness.

Almost the only point Korean cuisine shares in common with the cuisines of its larger neighbors - and indeed with the rest of Asia as well - is the vital role played by rice as the primary staple. "Have you eaten rice yet?" is a common greeting in both Chinese and Korean, roughly equivalent to the English "Hi, how are you?" The implication is that if you have then you must be feeling all right; and if you haven't, then you should be offered some forthwith.

First things first!

Koreans eat three full meals a day, and the number of dishes increases with each meal. At least half a dozen dishes appear with the traditional Korean breakfast, twice that number with lunch, and twenty or more at a full-scale banquet in the evening. Short grain rice is the staple at every meal, in the past often blended with barley or millet to stretch limited supplies. Like the Chinese and the Japanese, Koreans also eat noodles (sautéd or in soups), soy beans and bean curd, bean sprouts and red lentils. There the similarities end.

The most popular methods of cooking in Korea are communal "hot-pots" and the grilling of meat over charcoal or gas-fired braziers. Both methods reflect Mongol influence on Korean eating habits, and both permit cooking at

one's own table. Traditionally, diners sat on cushions on *ondol* floors around low, lacquered tables, and most Korean restaurants today still feature such charming *ondol* rooms as well as more contemporary table-and-chair set-ups. Implements comprise a long-handled, rather flat metal spoon, used for soups, stews and even rice, and a pair of slender metal chopsticks; dishes include a metal rice bowl with a lid, a soup bowl, and several small saucers for dips and garnishes.

ALL THE KIMCH'I YOU CAN EAT

The undisputed symbol of Korean cuisine is kimch'i, a term which refers to any side-dish which has been pickled in brine with garlic and chilies. There are more than twenty-four varieties of kim-

ch'i, each prepared in an infinite number of subtly different ways, and at least two or three versions appear with every meal. An old Korean adage has it that "A man can live without a wife, but not without his kimch'i, and only Seoul's most fanatically international restaurants fail to provide it. Practically every home in the country has rows of big black kimch'i pots fermenting away in backyard, porch or balcony.

Chili and garlic are the *sine qua non* of kimch'i; the most basic and widely-encountered variety calls for heads of fresh cabbage to be sliced, salted, placed in brine with plenty of chili and garlic, then set to ferment in those big pots. In summer, when fermentation is rapid and cabbages plentiful, kimch'i is made fresh daily; prior to the onset of winter the kimch'i pots are packed in straw and buried up to their necks in the ground to prevent freezing, then left to ferment for months.

Korean use of garlic goes back to prehistoric times. Chilies, on the other hand, are relative newcomers, having arrived on merchant ships from the Americas during the fifteenth and sixteenth centuries. Korea took to the fiery pods like fish to water.

The following are among the most popular varieties of kimch'i:

sobaegi kimch'i: cabbage stuffed with oysters;
oee sobaegi kimch'i: sliced cucumbers with radish and ginger;
kakdooki kimch'i: diced white radish with scallions;
dong chimi kimch'i: white radish sticks floating in brine.

Besides garlic and chili, favorite Korean seasonings include scallions, ginger, sesame oil, sesame seeds and soy sauce. Cooking herbs, which are applied according to the principles of tra-

A Korean meal is an attractive display and rare is one without at least some of the pickled side-dishes displayed in this lavish banquet setting,

throughout Korea, and are readily identified by the round holes set in the center of the tables to accommodate braziers.

A MEAL IN A BOWL

For simpler meals, especially for summer lunches, you could try one of the great Korean "single-bowl" meals. The best-known is *naeng-myon:* noodles of buckwheat or potato flour in cold broth, with sliced cucumber, pear-apple and pressed beef, topped with an egg and accompanied by a choice of seasonings. Other popular Korean noodle meals include the following:

momil kookso: buckwheat noodles with sweet radish sauce;
odaeng kookso: wheat noodles with fish cake in broth;
kong kookso: wheat noodles in fresh soy milk;
chap chae: thin rice noodles sautéd with meat and vegetables;
udong: broad wheat noodles with onions, bean curd, egg and chili.

If you would prefer a rice-based one-bowl meal, try asking for *hanjongshik*, which literally means "the meal of the day." This consists of a bowl of rice served with an array of fresh side dishes and a bowl of pickled cabbage soup. *Kongnamul pap* is a little fancier, with bean sprouts, beef and cabbage served over rice. The king of Korean rice dishes, however, is *pipimpap*, which is as much fun to eat as it is to pronounce. A big bowl of rice is topped with bean sprouts, bluebell root, blanched fern, spinach and a fried egg, and accompanied by a bowl of soup. Just mix it all up with your chopsticks and dig in.

One of the best Korean single-bowl meals is *samgyae tang*, which consists of a whole spring chicken stuffed with rice, white ginseng and dried jujubes, then steamed for hours in its own broth

in a heavy iron pot. More than just a meal, this dish is also a potent tonic food.

THE FOOD OF KINGS

There are two dishes, formerly reserved exclusively for Korean royalty, which dedicated gourmets will definitely wish to try while in Korea. *Kujolpan* ("Nine-treasure dish") comes in an octagonal lacquered dish with nine compartments. Delicate crepe skins fill the center compartment, surrounded by the other eight treasures: shredded egg, sautéd cucumbers, onions, mushrooms, beef, carrots, cabbage and shrimp. Just grab a crêpe skin and "roll your own."

The other royal delicacy is *sinsullo*, which comes in a brass pot with a chimney, much like a Mongolian firepot. Sliced beef with chopped onions and seasonings are placed in the bottom, with eggs, carrots, cucumbers, beef liver, chopped beef, blanched walnuts and fried ginko nuts neatly arranged on top. Live coals are then dropped into the chimney, while hot broth is poured over the ingredients. After a brief but vigorous simmering

quent excavation by archaeologists of ancient drinking cups and flasks attests. The ancient literature and painting are also full of boozing, and the habit proved the downfall of one Shilla dynasty king when soldiers from the neighboring Paekche kingdom surprised him and his courtiers during a party. The site at Kyongju, known as Posokjong (abalone bower) may still be viewed.

Drinking parties were formerly an exclusively male preserve, only *kisaeng* being excepted from the rule. This is changing rapidly, however, and Korean women seem to be developing as much of a taste for liquor as men.

Certain elements of traditional Korean etiquette are still observed by Koreans, particularly at formal parties, and foreigners who are clearly familiar with these customs will make a good impression. Never pour your own drink at a banquet, unless you wish to appear crude and greedy. Korean custom requires that you hold your glass before you (preferably with both hands) while your host, neighbor, waiter or *kisaeng* pours your drink for you. If someone toasts you and drains his glass, you are expected to follow suit. In this way many drinkers toast their way to oblivion, and this is absolutely normal and okay. No stigma attaches to drunkenness in Korea.

These are Korea's most popular drinks:

Soju: the common man's tipple, the cheapest and strongest Korean liquor, distilled from sweet potatoes or anything else that comes to hand; a taste which one is well advised not to go to too much trouble acquiring, as it can have a nasty kick the morning after; but goes well with Korean-style sausages and other meat dishes.

Makkolli: a milky, off-white brew, in taste akin to ginger beer, but more potent than it leads you to believe; formerly the nation's most popular drink, but rapidly losing out to beer. *Makolli* pubs, *makolli-jip,* used to be the most popular neighborhood bars, but in the big cities

it's ready to eat.

Meals in Korea are usually accompanied by teas of various sorts, mostly teas brewed from grains, dried fruits and ginseng. *Bori cha* (barley tea) is the commonest, and is served and drunk in place of water at every restaurant, coffee-shop and tea-room in the country. *Mogwa cha* (quince tea) and *hodo cha* (walnut tea) are other common varieties. *Insam cha* (ginseng tea) is a tonic drink imbibed the year round by Koreans of all ages. In recent years *kopi* (coffee), too, has become popular.

DRINKING: A NATIONAL PASTIME

Koreans like to drink, and there is no better way for the foreigner to get close to Koreans and find out what they are really thinking than by sharing a few glasses with them in a typical *sul-jip* (bar).

Drinking has always played an important part in Korean life from the King's court downwards, as the fre-

OPPOSITE Culinary time-travel at Suwon's Folk Village. ABOVE an artisan at the Folk Village makes candy in the traditional way.

flow into China, and if people there should adversely criticize them, how could we be without shame? Only types such as the Mongolians, Tanguts, Jurchen, Japanese and Tibetans have their own graphs, but these are matters for the barbarians..."

Fortunately for Korea, King Sejong persisted in his mission, and sparked enough interest among more enlightened scholars to prevent the *han'gul* from passing away in its infancy. In established literary circles, however, it remained subordinate to Chinese characters until the arrival of Christian missionaries in the nineteenth century. They were quick to see the merits of *han'gul* as a tool for disseminating knowledge to the masses, and as a result of their lead it soon became the universal way of representing the language. Han'gul survived suppression by the Japanese occupation, and nowadays is ubiquitous. Chinese ideograms are still taught in school and understood by all Koreans with a claim to culture, but their use in everyday life is very limited.

See **Travelers' Tips** for a list of basic Korean words and phrases, and for a note on romanization.

THE SEOUL OLYMPICS

There is little doubt that September 17, to October 2, 1988 will be the two most important weeks in the Republic of Korea's history to date. That's when some 13,000 athletes and officials, 9,000 journalists, 7,000 delegates and 270,000 foreign spectators are expected to descend on Seoul for the 24th Olympic Games.

It was in 1981 that the International Olympic Committee decided that the next Olympics after Los Angeles should go to Seoul, and the country has been undergoing paroxysms of preparation ever since. The capital's substrata has

been riddled with subway tunnels which now cover 116.5 km (72 miles) and one of the lines connects the Seoul Sports Complex, major venue for the Games, with the city center. The already well-developed expressway network was expanded and now one may travel from Seoul to anywhere in the country and be back in the capital the same day. A number of the stadiums and other facilities needed for the Games were already built and in use by 1981, but fifteen new ones had to be constructed from scratch, including the

huge main stadium of the Sports Complex, designed by celebrated Korean architect Kim Swoo-gun and opened in 1984. The finished complex comprises a baseball stadium, indoor swimming pool, two gymnasiums and a warm-up field in addition to the main stadium. It occupies an area of 54.5 hectares (135 acres) and has an overall capacity of 200,000. The main stadium alone can accommodate 100,000.

Seoul's other main venue, the Olympic Park, occupies a vast area four kilometers (two and a half miles) east of the complex along the south bank of the Han River and accommodates a velodrome, tennis courts, weightlifting and fencing gyms, a gymnastic hall, and an indoor swimming pool with a profile strongly suggestive of Admiral Yi's famous "turtle ships." The Olympic and Press village will be located here, and there will be about 50 hectares (135 acres) of greenery in the total area of 291 hectares (719 acres).

Seoul is very decidedly Korea's capital, and most of the Olympic events not scheduled for the Complex or the Park cities, Taegu, Kwangju and Taejon, will also host some events.

Besides the Games themselves, an ambitious Festival of Arts and Culture will be held around and during those weeks in autumn '88, including performances of Korean court and folk dance and music, concerts of Western classical music and exhibitions of Korean art treasures.

One of the biggest headaches for the organizers of the Olympics has been how to put all the visitors up. Already Seoul has fifty-four hotels of at least decent tourist standard, with over

will take place in other venues in the center or suburbs of the capital. The regatta course, for example, is on the Han River, 30 km (18.5 miles) east of Seoul; the modern pentathlon will take place in Taenung Country Club in the northeast of the city, while judo events will be held in Yong-In, an hour's drive to the south. A few events will be staged in other cities, however. Pusan, the nation's second city, will be the site of yachting events, and a mammoth coastal site is being built for that purpose. The municipal stadiums of the other major

12,000 rooms; by the time of the Games, some thirteen new ones will be in operation, with 4,000 rooms between them. Even so, a huge shortfall is anticipated, and to help fill the breach many local hotels and *yogwan* will be encouraged to upgrade their facilities to make them more suitable for foreign visitors. In addition, every available

OPPOSITE Participant in the opening ceremony of Seoul's Olympic stadium. ABOVE Athlete in the National Games putting in some practice for '88. OVERLEAF Panoramic view of the spectacular opening of the Asian Games in 1986.

type of housing, including condominiums, apartments, school dormitories and even private homes, will be pressed into service. There was even talk at one time of mooring a large ship at the port of Inch'on, and boarding surplus visitors there.

Koreans have been eager participants in the Olympics for decades. A Korean, Sohn Kee-chung, won the Marathon at Berlin in 1936, running for Japan, and since 1948, when they first took part under their own flag, they have done consistently well in boxing, weightlifting, judo, and more recently in wrestling, basketball, volleyball and archery as well. In Los Angeles they gave their best collective performance ever, ranking tenth in the final tally and collecting nineteen medals.

A political shadow hangs over the Olympics as it hangs over all Korea's international activities, and at the time of writing it was not clear to what extent the participation of the Eastern bloc countries in the Games could be anticipated. As a sop to North Korean feelings the suggestion has been made that some of the events might be held there.

Even if the Games is only a partial success in this respect, however, it will still have done great things for Korea's image and place in the world. The 1964 Tokyo Olympics, the only previous Games to be held in Asia, marked and was in large part responsible for a huge turnaround both in the world's attitude toward Japan and Japan's attitude to the rest of the world: once again the country seemed to have become part of the world community. The Seoul Olympiad is likely to have a similar effect. If it does, the US$2.25 billion it is likely to cost may be considered money well spent.

Official competitions will be held in twenty-three sports and demonstrations in two others. Of the official sports,

tennis and table tennis are new additions to the Olympic Games. The schedule of events is printed on the last page of this guide.

SPORT IN KOREA

The Olympics aside, sports of all kinds enjoy huge popularity in Korea, and the nation has made its impact felt in many international competitions. In particular, the reputation Koreans enjoy as one of the feistiest of Asian peoples is substantiated by their success in the martial arts, both eastern and western.

The indigenous martial art is *T'aekwondo*, "the Way of Feet and Fists," which has been practiced in the peninsula for the best part of two thousand years. It's an explosively dynamic fighting system in which the contestants concentrate all their energy, mental as well as physical, on assaulting carefully identified spots on the opponent's body. *T'aekwondo* is related to but distinct from both Chinese kung-fu and Okinawan karate and has in recent years gained wide international recognition. Now there are schools with Ko-

ABOVE Grecian wrestling at the National Games. Koreans excel in many of the martial arts, Western as well as Eastern, and embrace baseball OPPOSITE enthusiastically.

70

rean instructors dotted all over the globe. Koreans continue to win the majority of the titles at the regular international championships in which teams from more than sixty nations compete, and the sport has become one of the official events at the Asian Games. If you want to see a demonstration of the sport, contact the **World T'aekwondo Federation** at its headquarters in Kukkiwon, in the southern suburbs of Seoul, where regular exhibition bouts are staged. Call 776-2347 or 777-6080/9 for further information.

Yudo, judo to you, is the other oriental fighting art which has Korea in its grip. The "Way of Gentleness" was introduced into Korea from China in 1150, after which the Koreans taught it to the Japanese and then for many centuries lost interest in it. The Japanese brought it back with them during their occupation, and it is once again popular nationwide. It is part of the compulsory training of Korean policemen. It's not the only form of wrestling the Koreans go in for. *Ssirum*, a sport introduced by the Mongols, requires the hefty contestants to throw each each other to the ground, employing a strictly limited repertoire of trips, twists and flips; it bears a passing resemblance to Japanese sumo, and may often be seen at spring and autumn country festivals. Western-style wrestling has also had a large following since the Koreans took a gold for that event (featherweight free-style) at the 1976 Olympics. And boxing, where Koreans have excelled in the lighter categories for many years, approaches the status of a national sport.

The two most popular ball games in Korea are soccer and baseball. Baseball was professionalized several years ago, and the razzmatazz of the present-day game, and the long hours of television exposure it commands, are strongly reminiscent of the situation over the water in Japan. Koreans have been playing soccer ever since 1882, when the crew of a visiting British warship gave a demonstration of how it was done, and on both sides of the DMZ it is played avidly and with great skill. Both North and South Korean teams have in the past done remarkably well in the World Cup.

The
Broad
Highway

of it with a vast Korean banquet in the private room of a *kisaeng* house in Insa-dong.

Reminders of Korea's deep-seated problems are inescapable: the heights of the city's mountains still belong to the army, and the center is full of very young, very conspicuous plainclothes government security men. If you are here in May, when the university exams finish, you may be unlucky enough to catch a blast of tear gas wafting down from the city's campuses, where police will be breaking up yet another protest by students at the snail-like pace of the nation's progress toward democratic government. But equally, the rude vigor and confidence of the country are evident everywhere, too; the tall, aggressive new buildings sprouting on every block that have transformed the city's looks in the past decade; the press of fashionable, prosperous youth through the streets of Myong-dong, where the boutiques and department stores are concentrated.

GETTING STARTED

Administratively speaking, Seoul is a "special city," with the same status as a

province. The city is divided into sixteen *gu* or wards, each of which is further divided into *dong* or precincts. Main roads are divided by length into *ka*, sections. However, knowing the exact address of where you want to go does not necessarily guarantee that you will find it. As new roads and buildings are superimposed on the city's essentially medieval layout, the streets and lanes of Seoul form an ever-more complex maze, especially since all new construction must now be designed around the old palaces, shrines, city gates and so on which have been declared national monuments. To compound the problem, house numbers are not assigned in logical, sequential order but according to the date the house was built. So the best way to get around Seoul on your own is to memorize a few major landmarks and then work your way to specific destinations from there.

Probably the single most useful point for the visitor to orientate him or herself to is the main hotel district, with the Lotte and Chosun Hotels at its center. From here you are only a few steps away from City Hall, Toksu Palace and the bustling Myong-dong shopping and pleasure district (all described below). The single word "It'aewon" will be enough to get you to that vital part of town, reached through the tunnels that pierce Namsan (South Mountain). To reach the colorful markets of eastern Seoul, as well as Seoul Stadium and its mass of sporting goods shops, the key word is **Tongdaemun, "Great East Gate."**

For visitors in the city for a matter of days or weeks, taxis, subway and feet are certainly the best ways to get around. Taxis become a problem in the evening when everyone wants to ride them and there are simply not enough to go round, because (it is said) of the restriction on gasoline imports (Korea still has one of the world's largest foreign debts). Unless you shout your destination clearly as the cabs cruise past, you risk being left

stranded by the side of the road for-ever. If several fares are going in the same direction the driver will take them all, though you will usually still have to pay the amount shown on the meter. Larger "call taxis" are more often available because their fares start at ₩1,000 instead of the normal ₩600. For wealthy you they are a sen-sible alternative to hanging about. You can either book them by special road-side phones or hail them if they are cruising.

If you stay in the city longer than a few weeks, or if you are taken around by a Korean friend, you may start rid-ing the buses. This is not recommended for solitary newcomers because desti-nations are only written in *han'gul*. To take a bus, first buy a token (₩120) at one of the many kiosk stores on the main streets - these are always found close to bus stops. Alternatively pay ₩130 in cash. In either case you pay as you enter. People waiting for buses in Seoul do not form lines but mill around in the general area then make a con-certed dash for the door when it arrives. Great fun.

CITY SIGHTS

The word Seoul means "capital," and its history as such begins in 1392 when King T'aejo established the Yi dynasty here, usurping the power of the Koryo dynasty which had been based in Kaesong, now a short way over the border in North Korea. It has remained the pre-eminent city ever since, though frequently threatened and more than once destroyed by invaders. The strongest reminders of how the city must have looked in the past are its gates: five of the original nine remain (though not all in their original loca-tions). Formerly they were linked by a ten-mile wall of earth and dressed stone which was the city's boundary, only fragments of which survive to-day, some on Pugak-san, the mountain on the city's north side, some on Nam-san, the mountain which is now close to the city's center. The modern city flows way beyond the area which the

The trendy lady in It'aewon, ABOVE, and the para-gon of traditional virtue, OPPOSITE, might just be the same person.

Korea's official Chogye sect of Buddhism and the administrative center of 1,500 affiliated temples throughout the country. Located in the central Insa-dong area, it is walkable from the central hotel district. Though always colorful and humming with pious activity, by far the best time to visit Chogye-sa (*sa* means "temple") is on Buddha's birthday, which falls on the eighth day of the fourth lunar month (usually early or mid-May). This auspicious event is celebrated with great fanfare at Chogye-sa and other Buddhist temples around the country. On the eve of the holiday the faithful purchase paper lanterns to which they attach long streamers inscribed with the names of their family members. Illuminated by little candles, these are hung by the hundred in the temple grounds, and as evening falls the worshipers chant prayers for a prosperous and peaceful year to come. Women dressed in billowy, pastel *hanbok* crowd the courtyards, adding color and cacophony to the scene, and the air fills with simultaneously conducted sutra-chanting and Western choral singing. Many foreign residents of Seoul participate in this annual celebration by purchasing and hanging paper lanterns of their own. Why not you? The cost, which is basically a contribution to the temple, runs to about ₩10,000.

Tongdaemun and Namdaemun

The Great East and Great South Gates are the two of Seoul's five ancient city gates which have survived to the present. These fine examples of traditional Korean architecture, pockmarked by shells from the Korean War, do not really require that you make a special trip to go and see them, but they are convenient landmarks for the city's two biggest and most fantastic markets, also called Tongdaemun and Namdaemun. For more about these, see the following section.

SHOPPING IN SEOUL

Seoul is one of the best places in the world for shopping, and many visitors come for no other reason. Whether it is traditional Korean products such as antique chests, celadon, silk and ginseng that appeal, or contemporary items such as clothes, calculators, watches and sports accessories, Seoul offers a wide range of high-quality products, often at ridiculously reasonable prices.

There are a number of major shopping districts in the city, and each tends to specialize in certain types of products.

These are Korea's most popular products, followed by a list of the best shopping districts:

Ginseng, Korea's first export, is available here in all its many forms: dried roots, liquid extract, powder, capsules, candied slices, instant tea, soap,

ABOVE Statue of nationalist hero Kim Ku in Seoul's Namsan Park. OPPOSITE the Capitol Building, constructed by the Japanese, behind Kwanghwa-mun Gate. OVERLEAF In Seoul the desolate, craggy mountains are never far away.

shampoo, skin cream and cigarettes. A box of fifty five-year-old roots of white ginseng currently retails for about $50 in Seoul. Red ginseng is more potent, more expensive and more difficult to find. Because ginseng is a state monopoly, prices are fixed nationwide, so have no qualms about buying ginseng at any place you happen to find it.

Silk is another famous Korean product that goes back a long way, and experienced fabric shoppers will quickly recognize the great silk bargains that are to be found in Seoul. Today, most American department stores buy their finished silk products wholesale in Korea, and even Thailand imports considerable quantities of raw silk to make its famous polished "Thai silk" products. Korean silk comes in an incredible variety of colors and patterns, both in prints and brocades, and it is suitable for clothing as well as decorative use. If the item you want is a mixture of silk and synthetics, it should be considerably cheaper than the pure silk equivalent.

Seoul's largest selection of silk in bulk is found in the **Tongdaemun Market**, where hard bargaining is the order of the day. Start your bidding low, roll your eyes in outrage at the counter-offer, raise your bid a bit, threaten to take your business elsewhere, and so forth, until you've struck a good bargain. For ready-made silk clothing, the boutiques of Myong-dong and the hotel arcades are good places to shop.

Korean Ceramics have been highly praised for centuries for quality of craftsmanship and originality of design. Celadon, with its distinctive blue-green glaze and white inlaid designs, is by far the most famous product of Korean kilns. Although all the best celadon was made more than 600 years ago, before the Yi dynasty, contemporary potters make excellent reproductions of this as well as of delicate white Yi dynasty porcelain and the earthy pots of the Shilla period with their characteristic perforated legs. The sort of items available include stemmed wine cups, long-necked wine decanters, tea-cups and tea pots, incense burners, vases and decorative bowls.

The best-known and most accessible area to buy ceramics, antique chests and furniture is **Insa-dong**, near the center of town, but prices are steep, partly reflecting the high rents here. Much the cheapest and most interesting place to buy antique pots as well as chests, old silk clothing and other antiques is **Changan-dong**, a taxi ride out to the east of the city center. The first floors of two adjacent buildings are full of little antique shops, and as the goods overflow onto the street the buildings are easy to spot. Dealers will try to persuade you that their Shilla-style pots really are 1,500 years old, and that they are often believed is a tribute to the innocence of their customers. But there are plenty of bargains around for the discriminating.

New ceramics are available in every arcade and department store in Seoul, but be forewarned: blue-green celadon

cient Great East Gate on Chongno Street, this is the biggest market in Korea. Spread over ten city blocks, the "Great East Gate Market" is divided into a number of buildings, each of which specializes in different types of products.

The main building, six stories high and two blocks long, is where you'll find the best bargains in Korean silk and synthetic brocades. Row upon row of little stalls, their bolts of fabric spilling colorfuly into the aisles, vie for the attention of passing shoppers. Here you can purchase traditional *hanbok* costumes ready-made, for men and women, silk fabric in bulk, buttons, zippers, pendants and other tailoring accessories, embroidered quilt-covers, bedspreads, pillow-cases and attractive floor-cushions. With a bit of bargaining you can really obtain some good buys in this sprawling market-place. Of course it is always best to take along a Korean acquaintance to a place like this, but basic English, the few vital questions listed in **Travelers' Tips** and sign language will be enough to see you through.

The other side of the elevated highway from the main market hall is another massive building which specializes in ready-made casual wear, shoes, sandals and sundry household items. The shops in the vicinity of the nearby Seoul Stadium sell every conceivable variety of sports clothing and athletic equipment at bargain prices. There are other shopping arcades both above and below ground. It's a vast emporium.

It'aewon: Ever since the Japanese invasions of 1592-98, during which many Japanese soldiers married Korean women and settled down here, It'aewon has been Seoul's major foreign enclave. Today it is a lively avenue of clothing shops, tailors, restaurants, coffee-shops, bars and night clubs, all of which are geared towards the tastes and budgets of American GIs stationed at Yongsan.

For export-quality contemporary cloth-

ing, It'aewon is the best place in Seoul to shop. Such stores as Muriel's Sweater Shop offer the latest in sports shirts, blouses, sweaters and other garments at remarkably low prices. Jackets, belts, bags, wallets, shoes and other leather and eelskin items are good value here. There are also shops which specialize in brassware, lacquerware, antique reproductions and souvenirs. Almost all proprietors in It'aewon speak sufficiently good English to conduct business with foreign customers.

An interesting local open-air market runs parallel to the south side of the main street, in a long alley just behind the clothing shops and tailors. Here you'll find local produce, cooking utensils and household items for sale, as well as little eateries specializing in various types of Korean snack food.

Department Stores: Seoul's major department stores are as big and modern as anything in the West, and they should definitely be included on any serious shopper's itinerary. Located in and around Myong-dong, they offer at fixed prices the whole range of consumer products manufactured in Korea.

The biggest of them is the **Lotte Shopping Center**, next door to the Lotte Hotel. Start your browsing in the basement of the food department, where the array of Korean and Western culinary products is incredible. Bakery items are especially good. The next seven floors are devoted to the usual sort of products stocked by department stores everywhere. The eighth floor is entirely given over to a duty-free shop for tourists, and is divided into a section for Korean products and one for brand-name luxury items imported from abroad. The ninth and ten floors have been dubbed "Food Street," and accommodate two dozen restaurants offering everything from oriental to western cuisine and from snacks to feasts.

These are the names, addresses, phone numbers and official weekly holidays of Seoul's major department stores:

Lotte Shopping Center, 1 Sokong-dong, Chung-gu. Tel: 771-25 (Tuesday).

Yol (mattresses) and *ibol* (bedspreads) in lurid abundance at a store in Tongdaemun.

Midopa Department Store, 123, 2-ka, Namdaemun-ro, Chung-gu. Tel: 754-2222 (No holiday).
Shinsegae Department Store, 51-2, 1-ka, Chungmu-ro, Chung-gu. Tel: 754-1234 (Monday).
Cheil Department Store, 31-1, 2-ka Myong-dong, Chung-gu. Tel: 776-2741 (Thursday).
Cosmos Department Store, 83-5, 2-ka Myong-dong, Chung-gu. Tel: 776-2601 (Tuesday).

Shopping Arcades: Seoul's shopping arcades are among the most extensive in Asia. Major downtown hotels such as the Chosun, Lotte and Seoul Plaza each have their own arcades of shops, which sell everything from celadon, silk and ginseng to cameras, waches, cosmetics and Western fashions. Despite the expensive ambiance, the prices as well as the quality of many items are broadly comparable with those sold in the department stores and other arcades.

Many of the underground passageways used by pedestrians to cross Seoul's main streets serve as vast shopping arcades, especially in the downtown area. Seoul's major shopping arcades are:

Underground:
Bando Chosun (below the Chosun Hotel).
Lotte First Avenue (below Lotte Hotel and Shopping Center).
Sokong (adjacent to Bando Chosun Arcade).
Ulchi (beneath Ulchi Road, 2-ka).
Chonggak (beneath Chongno Road, 2-ka)
Haehyon (beneath Namdaemun Road, near Great East Gate).

Above ground:
Seun (along Chongno Road, 4-ka).
Sampung (along Ulchi Road, 4-ka).
Tongbang Building Arcade.
Daewoo Building Arcade.

Duty-Free Shops: Seoul has a number of special duty-free shops and "Foreign Commissaries" exclusively for the use of foreign shoppers. The former sell Western luxury items and liquor as well as local handicrafts. You can use either local or foreign currencies, but you must show your passport. Duty-free shops are located at **Kimp'o International Airport**, the **Lotte Shopping Center, eighth floor**, the Nam Moon Shop (5 Yang-dong, Chung-ku), **Ungchon Company** (15 Insa-dong, Chongro-gu), the **Dong-wha Shop** (1-41 Sajik-dong, Chongro-ku), **Hotel Shilla, Hanjin** (at Seoul Station) and **Diamond** (at Mugyo-dong. Foreign Commissaries stock common American foods such as peanut butter, cheese-spread, potato chips etcetera, as well as toiletries and other items. Both tourists and foreign residents may shop in these commissaries, which are located in the Chosun Hotel arcade, the Lotte basement arcade, Myong-dong, and elsewhere about town.

SEOUL BY NIGHT

Seoul is an industrious city, but by no means a puritanical one. When the working day is done they put their work ethics away in their briefcases, loosen their ties and go mad. You can go mad, too, and stay that way as long as you like.

It wasn't always thus. Until 1981 a strictly imposed midnight curfew lent a quality of desperation to the city's night life, especially towards 11:30 pm, when revelers poured their drinks down their throats, rushed about in a last-minute search for companions, then scrambled back to homes or hotels before the witching hour struck. Since it has been lifted, however, the nervous tension has happily dissipated, and today Seoul can boast one of Asia's most colorful and varied night scenes, with something for every taste and budget.

Whether you are seeking Western- or Korean-style entertainment, a modern or traditional ambiance, low-budget beer halls and tea-rooms or high-rolling nightclubs and casinos, Seoul has them all. For the reader's convenience, this section is divided into two parts, Western-style and Korean-style. Bear in mind that whatever you find in Seoul after dark will have its equivalents elsewhere in the country; once you've mastered the scene here, other cities are a breeze.

Western Style

If you like to begin the evening with cocktails, the bars of the leading hotels will get you off to the best start. The most enduringly popular is the **Ninth Gate Bar** in the lobby of the Westin Chosun Hotel, which has good live music. Another popular spot is the painfully named **Bobby London Pub** in the lower arcade of the Lotte Hotel. Alternatively try the **Banjul**, which also has live music and a good Western restaurant and hostess club on its upper floors. The Banjul is located two lanes behind the Samilro Building. Single men might like to start the evening with a few drinks at the **Tiger House**, diagonally opposite the Chosun Hotel, or at the Savoy Hotel's **Goody-Goody Bar**, located in the basement.

Seoul's history as a cosmopolitan city only goes back a few years, and the most reliable places to eat good European and American food are still the international hotels. Each of Seoul's leading deluxe hotels has at least one good gourmet restaurant featuring Western cuisine, and though prices tend to be high, the culinary standards and the service may be said to justify it. Seoul's first gourmet French restaurant was the Chosun's **Ninth Gate**, and it still re-

OPPOSITE Bridges over Seoul's Han River at dusk.

mains in favor. Its decor strikes a good balance between opulence and restraint, and the menu offers traditional favorites as well as innovative house specialties.

Of the thirty-one restaurants and bars operated by the Lotte Hotel, the **Prince Eugene** provides the most splendid luxury. Its palatial decor is matched by one of the most impressive menus in town - and some of the highest prices. For a more subdued ambiance try the Hyatt Regency's **Hugo's Restaurant**, a fine continental restaurant with a well-founded reputation, or perhaps the **Celadon Restaurant** on the second floor of the Sheraton Walker Hill, where the food is complemented by celadon and German crystal. Buffet enthusiasts will find Seoul's most bountiful buffet table, groaning with Western as well as Japanese and Korean selections, at the Shilla Hotel's **Shangri-la Restaurant**, built into a wing of the old Yi dynasty guest-house there. If you

fancy a steak cooked the American way, try the **El Toro** on the second floor of the Seoul Plaza Hotel.

If you wish to escape from the hotels and their prices, there are a few places on the outside which serve good Western food in pleasant surroundings. **La Cantina** (tel: 771-2579), located directly across from the Lotte Hotel in the basement of the Sam Sung Building, serves authentic Italian cuisine at reasonable prices and is quite popular with Seoul's resident foreign community. Or maybe you would like to rub shoulders with Korea's most popular entertainers, many of whom dine Western-style at the **Hee Joon** (tel: 265-1466), a cosy dinner club with live music in the basement of the Kuk-dong Building.

What next? How about a show? Seoul has a number of interesting theater-restaurants, which feature excellent entertainment but only mediocre cooking. The best idea is to eat elsewhere and arrive in time for the show, which usually begins around 8 pm. The **Kayagum Theater Restaurant** at the Sheraton walker Hill stages the most extravagant floor shows in town. The

night begins with a thoroughly vulgarized presentation of traditional Korean music and dance, but after the horsehair hatted band calls it quits, looking understandably grumpy, the real fun begins. The Western part of the show - truly Western, almost all the performers being either European or American - is elaborately staged and slickly enjoyable for anyone who has been away from this sort of thing for a time. It's topless but harmless, so don't feel shy about going *à deux*.

The Sheraton Walker Hill also has the only casino in Seoul, one of the eleven in the country, each located at a different tourist center. Only non-Koreans are allowed to gamble at these casinos.

Connoisseurs of classical music should try to catch a concert, opera or symphony while in Seoul. The standards are high, and a number of Korean musicians have attained international fame. The **Sejong Cultural Center**, located opposite the American Embassy on Sejong Road, and the **National Theater**, home of Korea's National Ballet, National Symphony and Na-

tional Opera, both stage regular performances featuring well-known Korean as well as international musicians, singers and dancers. For current programs and schedules call the Korean Culture and Arts Foundation (tel: 741-0051)

If you prefer pop music, the best place in central Seoul may well be **OB's Cabin** (tel: 776-4784), a four-floor music club popular with Seoul's foreign community. It's in the heart of Myong-dong, two lanes behind UNESCO House. **All that Jazz** (tel: 792-5701), at 168-17 It'aewon-dong, is Seoul's best jazz club, with American disc-jockeys and live jam sessions three times a week.

Most of Seoul's big hotels have discotheques. The Lotte's **Annabelle's**, the Chosun's **Club Tomorrow** and the Shilla's **Club Universe** are all very popular, as are the discos at the Hyatt and Sheraton Walker Hill. Another good dancing club is the **Club Copa-**

ABOVE It'aewon at night. Discos upstairs, stalls selling snacks on the street below.

wears on. **All that Jazz**, mentioned above, is across the road and a little way down the hill from the Sportsman's. The steep, narrow lane behind the Sportsman's, known variously as GI Alley or the Village, is lined with bars and clubs of various shapes and sizes where the mixture of country-and-western music, paunchy, aging

cabana (tel: 777-2947), located in a narrow lane behind Tiffany's, with two floors of dancing and American DJs. Seoul's disco clubs are equally enjoyable for couples and for singles, and unattached guests usually have no problem finding partners.

It'aewon, however, is much the best and most interesting place to dance in Seoul. There are several discos along the main road; entrance is usually free, drinks are cheaper than in the big hotels, and the It'aewon atmosphere is unique if a little weird. Most of the foreigners are male and military, while most of the girls are lithe young locals eager for a brush with the big world and happy to dance all night in exchange for a few beers. The best-known place is the **Sportsman's Club**, though others such as the **UN Tourist Club**, **King Club** and **Servicemen's Club** also warm up as the evening

military men and young Korean hostesses showing off their incredible legs in hot pants is piquant to say the least. Presence of mind is useful when moseying around in this part of town as daydreamers are liable to get yanked clean off the street by hookers not known for their subtlety. If you do sit down with a hostess in one of these clubs, you will naturally be expected to replenish her glass of colored water (and your own of whiskey or beer) at frequent intervals, but prices are reasonable by international standards. Beware, however, of catching something you can't get rid of. Be prepared.

Korean Style
Koreans, too, like to start a night on the town with a few quiet drinks, and in

Night scenes in It'aewon. ABOVE LEFT and OPPOSITE LEFT a few graphic arguments for learning to read Han'gul. ABOVE RIGHT It'aewon's foreigners are mostly though not exclusively military. OPPOSITE RIGHT Night scene at Lotte's open-air restaurant, central Seoul.

Seoul there is no shortage of places to sample. Myong-dong and other districts of downtown Seoul are full of Korean taverns and restaurants, and most of them can easily be identified by sight. Starting with the simplest, you could try a small bottle of *soju*, the sweet potato distillation which is the favorite of serious Korean drinkers, at one of the local bars, small, noisy, smoke-filled taverns where ruddy-faced workers exchange boisterous toasts while snacking on excellent *anju*. *Chogae* (clams grilled on the half-shell) and *sogum-gui* (grilled beef) are enduring *anju* favorites. Even simpler than such places are the *pojang-macha*, tent wagons with red, white and blue awnings located in alleys and byways all over Seoul. The

one that often comes to rest in the alley next to the Samilro Building can be recommended.

A step up from *soju* is *makkolli*, a cloudy rice brew which was traditionally Korea's most popular drink. **Tae Ryon** (tel: 265-5439) and **Chonggey-Oke** (tel: 267-2744), both located across the street from the Samilro Building, are typical *makkolli* houses

which serve particularly tasty *anju*. Behind the new high-rises at the Kwanghwamun intersection, each with a blue "Jinro Limited" sign over the door, stand four *makkolli* houses in a row, where you can drink *yakchu* (highly-refined *makkolli*) and sample the excellent *pindaetok* (shrimp-studded, mung bean pancakes) and *chogaetang* (clam soup).

For foreigners, the most popular type of Korean drinking establishment seems to be the beer-hall, where chilled draft beer (*saeng maekju*), usually "OB" brand, and simple snacks are served. Small and cozy, beer-halls can grow quite lively. They are easily identified by square red signs with a frothy mug of beer inside a white ring. **Blue Villa** (tel: 23-3694) is one of numerous beer-halls located within a single block behind the Seoul Plaza Hotel in the direction of South Gate. There are plenty in Myong-dong, too - just keep walking until you come across one that strikes your fancy.

Another modern sort of Korean bistro is the "stand bar," where customers sit at a long bar while hostesses serve

narrow passageway just behind the Commercial Bank of Korea off Myong-dong's main drag. Accompanied by a few shots of Jinro Ginseng Wine and topped off with a glass of fresh-squeezed ginseng juice, this meal is a marvelous example of the great Far Eastern tradition of blending food and medicine.

Of course it is possible to sample the full range of Korean cuisine at the fancy (and rather expensive) restaurants in the major hotels. The Shilla's **Sora-bol** and the Lotte's **Mugunghwa** serve traditional Korean fare in elegant sur-roundings, and English menus are available. At **Po Suk Jung** in B1 floor of the Lotte Hotel, the traditional meal is accompanied by a pocket-sized but skillful display of Korean dancing and music. Or you could opt for an evening at Korea House (see below), where the program of dancing and drama may be preceded by dinner either buffet-style or around a low lacquered table.

The ultimate dining experience in Seoul - one which combines traditional food, drink and entertainment within the context of classical Korean culture - is an evening at a *kisaeng* house, an ex-perience which requires a considerable outlay of cash. Comparable in style and content to Japan's geisha houses, though less formal, the *kisaeng* house experience gives a fair idea of what it must have been like to be a moneyed aristocrat in the old days. The cost usu-ally comes to about US$50-70 per per-son for food and drinks, plus another $30 or so in tips for the ladies who ac-company guests throughout dinner, so count on spending about $100 per head.

Unless you happen to speak fluent Korean it's always advisable to visit a *kisaeng* house in the company of at least one Korean friend, otherwise you'll miss most of the fun. Your party will have its own private dining-room decorated in classical Korean fashion, and you will be served by a bevy of at-tractive young *kisaeng* clad in colorful Korean dress, who will pour your drinks, wipe your brow and generally keep you amused.

If you happen to establish a rapport with one of the girls during the eve-ning, you may feel free to ask her out; she is under no obligation to accept, and if she does, her fee is bound to be high. Your Korean friend will act as in-termediary, and he in turn will consult the house's *mama-san*, who makes all decisions and sets all the fees. On the other hand, if you are with a mixed group, don't hesitate to bring your own spouse or date to a *kisaeng* house; they're quite as happy to welcome mixed parties as all-male groups.

Seoul's most renowned and exclusive *kisaeng* house is **Sam Cheong Gak** (tel: 762-0151/59), a beautiful walled gar-den compound with a palatial ban-queting hall and pavilions in a land-scaped garden setting.

Accustomed to hosting foreign par-ties, the Sam Cheong Gak can handle groups of a hundred or more with equal ease. Another popular *kisaeng* house is the **Jang Won** (tel: 72-8645), located about 65 meters in front of the police box behind the US Embassy.

For a more contemporary though only slightly less expensive version of the *kisaeng* house, try a contemporary Korean salon. The service is essentially the same, but the setting is modern: ta-bles and chairs instead of *ondol* floors, hostesses in gowns instead of *hanbok*. Salons abound in Seoul, and are easily identified by the word "salon" in Eng-lish over the door.

The most extraordinary relic of Seoul's traditional night-life scene, one which will perhaps be lucky to survive the preparations for the Olympics but

Shows and Concerts

For an introduction to traditional music and dance, the government-sponsored **Korea House**, near the northern slopes of Namsan, is hard to beat. Set in an attractive garden, the traditionally-styled center has a nightly program of stage entertainment which includes shaman rituals, mask-dance drama and solos on classical instruments. In addition, free performances of folk dancing are given every Saturday and Sunday at 3 pm. There is a library of films which can be viewed on request, and a bookstand with a good selection of English-language publications about Korea. A restaurant serves traditional cuisine, and you may opt to eat either buffet-style in a dining-room with tables and chairs, or cross-legged in a private *ondol* room, served by waitresses in *hanbok*. The phone numbers of Korea House are 266-9101/4 and 267-8752.

The Sejong Cultural Center, mentioned above, right in the heart of the city and within view of the Capitol Building, was completed in 1978 and represents an early, groping attempt to find an architectural style that is both modern and Korean. The resulting slightly fascist look is a pity. The large hall has a ninety-nine-rank organ and performances of symphonies, plays and other works are frequently given. Along with the National Theater, this is one of the city's most important venues for top artists, both Korean and non- Korean.

TRADITIONAL INNS *(YOGWAN)*

For a stay at one of the few *yogwan* which retain the atmosphere of an earlier age, try the **Un Dang Yogwan**. A short way south of Changdok Palace and tricky to find unaided, it is buried away in one of the few central sections of town which has yet to feel the dead hand of development. Un Dang Yogwan (tel: 765-4194/7) was formerly the house of a nobleman, and the organiza-

tion of its many discrete parts, folded in on each other like an oversize game of dominoes, reflects that history. Raised above the ground on large stones, the larger pavilions originally accommodated the wealthy owner and his immediate family, while the smaller rooms to the side were reserved for retainers, parasites and poets. All are now part of the *yogwan*, and whichever you choose it is guaranteed to delight: the demerara-colored floors, the delicate woodwork and hand-made translucent paper, the surprising little gardens at every turn, the sumptuous traditional breakfast, and above all the uncanny tranquility of the place, all combine to make this unlike any other accommodation in the world. The Un Dang is not Seoul's most convenient accommodation, and can be far from tranquil at night when some of the guests have a party. Bathrooms are communal and the only air-conditioning is an electric fan. But few inns anywhere in the country offer a comparably rich experience of the traditional way of life.

In the narrow streets behind the Sejong Center are some of the *yogwan* which are most popular with young for-

eign travelers, as well as a number of good, moderately-priced restaurants. The two best-known *yogwan* are **Inn Daewon** (tel: 735-7891) and **Inn Daeji** (tel: 737-4659). These are good places to stay if you are desperate for company and chat, or want to exchange information about traveling cheap elsewhere in the country.

THE GRAND HOTELS

Like the rest of the country, Seoul has no shortage of accommodation, though for a crucial couple of weeks in 1988 that statement may be open to question. There are hotels and inns to suit every pocket and predilection, from simple inns and the traditional *yogwan* described above on page 104, through efficient if flavorless concrete boxes and the gloomily genteel YMCA, to the five-star international hotels. Of the latter there are seven, and as much of the city's social life, for Western residents as well as visitors, continues to revolve around

OPPOSITF The towers of the Lotte Hotel, set off by a Yi dynasty pavilion which belongs to neighboring Westin Chosun Hotel. ABOVE Dinner show in Lotte Hotel's Po Suk Jung Restaurant.

them, here are profiles of each. A list of other, less expensive hotels in Seoul and elsewhere is provided in **Travelers' Tips**.

Westin Chosun
Seoul's most famous international hotel, the Chosun opened its doors for business a full decade before its competitors, and since then has established an excellent reputation both with travelers and locally resident businessmen. If you are the type who prefers a quiet hotel with personal service and a somewhat old-fashioned atmosphere, choose the Chosun.

Among the Chosun's facilities are an outdoor swimming-pool, a rooftop buffet restaurant with fine views and a night club. But its most popular attraction is the **Ninth Gate Bar and Restaurant**, favorite international rendezvous. The bar's plate-glass windows look out on another unique Chosun feature, an old Yi dynasty pavilion, a registered national treasure, set in the midst of the Chosun's garden. Next to the bar is the Ninth Gate Restaurant, Seoul's first gourmet French restaurant and still one of the best.

The **Chosun** is located right in the center of the city, with convenient access by foot to major business, government and shopping centers. Most guests are "FITs," foreign individual travelers, rather than tour groups, so even when the hotel is full it rarely seems crowded or noisy. Average room rates run at about $110 a night, while suites are between $275 and $800.

Lotte
With close on a thousand rooms, the Lotte is Seoul's largest hotel: It has an enormous marble lobby, and a lobby lounge serving coffee and cocktails which looks out on a spectacular artificial waterfall. The Lotte's **Peninsula Coffee Shop** does a terrific and very popular buffet breakfast.

103

cipitous drop away from It'aewon. Among its many facilities are a large outdoor pool, a health club, a disco and a branch of **Hugo's**, Hyatt's restaurant chain.

The hotel is organized along standard Hyatt lines, which means the rooms are rather smaller than elsewhere and the atmosphere less distinctive. Frequent international travelers, however, may find the Hyatt attractive on account of the many conveniences this large international chain can provide. Rates are about the same as at the Shilla.

Sheraton Walker Hill

This is the most secluded of Seoul's major hotels as it is a good twenty minutes' drive from the center of town, in the midst of elaborately landscaped grounds. It is a large hotel, with 770 rooms and many recreational facilities, including indoor and outdoor pools, jogging and hiking trails, tennis courts, a nightclub and numerous restaurants.

The **Sheraton** has two major claims to fame: its theater-restaurant (see **Seoul By Night** for details) and its casino, the only one in Seoul. Due to its distance from downtown, the Sheraton's rates are the lowest of the major hotels, ranging from $70 to $115 a double room.

Seoul Hilton

The newest of the major hotels, the Seoul Hilton is located near the Great South Gate on the lower slopes of Mt Namsan and opened in 1983. The 629-room hotel has a fantastic lobby and Korean touches to the decor of the rooms. Facilities include an indoor swimming pool, an athletic club, top-floor executive suites with concierge, and a number of first-class restaurants. The center of town is about five minutes away by taxi. Room rates average about $95 a night.

SEOUL AREA SIDE-TRIPS

There is so much to see and do in Seoul that it is hard to drag oneself away, but the effort should be made. Even if you lack the time to travel further afield, there are a number of places close to the capital which can add quite a new dimension to your experience of the country. Each of the destinations described below may be visited from Seoul in the space of a day, though one or two merit an overnight stay if you can spare the time.

Korea is arguably one of the easiest countries in the world to travel around in. Tours are available to some of the best-known destinations - and the *only* way to see P'anmunjom in the Demilitarized Zone is on an official tour - but the traveler who treasures his freedom will be glad to know that in Korea independent travel is a piece of cake. Buses go everywhere, with unbelievable frequency (and sometimes great videos en route, too; *Dracula versus Billy the Kid* was one recent offering). Trains are dependable and comfortable. Highways are new and swift and remarkably under-used due to the high price of gas, and while a rented car is much the most expensive way to see the country, it may be the best if you're in a tearing hurry.

KOREAN FOLK VILLAGE

Perhaps you've already seen the waxworks of traditional Koreans in reconstructed environments inside the Folk Museum at Kyongbok Palace. **The Korean Folk Village** at Suwon, 51 km (32 miles) south of Seoul, takes the visitor an important step closer to understanding how traditional, rural Korea looked, smelled and tasted, the sort of spaces it felt at home in, where it locked up its criminals, and what it liked to do on its day off.

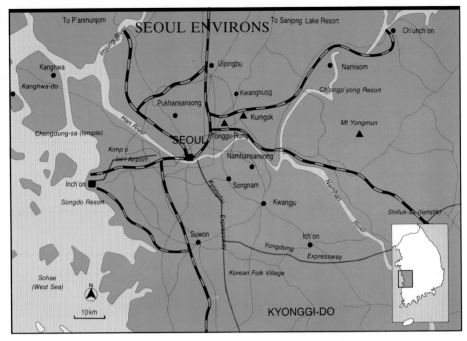

Girdled by wooded hills in the countryside, twenty minutes by bus or taxi from the town of Suwon, the village comprises 240 cottages, villas, administrative offices, taverns and other buildings, as well as a lake, a stream, a bridge, an open-air performance space and abundant tea shops and restaurants. Many of the buildings date back to the Yi dynasty, having been transported from far and near and then reconstructed; even those that are of more recent date at least *look* that old.

But the folk village is more than a museum of old buildings, for in many of them you can see craftspeople, not waxworks this time, at work in the old way. Here's a carpenter, pulling the plane towards him as he smoothes a plank. Under the eaves of that cottage two women are spinning silk from the cocoons bubbling in a cauldron. Elsewhere you'll see blacksmiths forging traditional tools with hammer and anvil, a scholar practicing calligraphy in his study, a young woman wearing *hanbok* pounding rice into flour in an old stone mortar. The criminals in the

jail and the cows in the cow shed are fakes - but the chickens strutting officiously around are for real, as is the priest who takes care of the Buddhist temple. A pounding of drums draws you to the dirt ring near the center of the village where you find a big crowd gathered to watch a vivid folk dance, the boys with paper tapes flying from their caps swirling round and round the space like toy tops.

The folk village is a theme park in a sense, a huge open-air drama which takes place simultaneously on dozens of different stages. But what gives it the edge on Disneyland is that it's almost for real. The craftspeople, one senses, are perfectly at home with their tasks: those women spinning silk have surely been doing it all their lives. And it's not only the performers who seem natural and at home here; the visitors, the great majority Korean, may be wearing Western clothes, but they are a generation or less away from these traditional realities. Young girls attack the bouncing see-saw with hilarious abandon, their elders sit and fan themselves on the ve-

randahs of old cottages, or tackle feasts of *anju* and great bowls of *makkolli* in the taverns at the far end of the site. After a while any sense of distance between visitors and village evaporates.

The Folk Village is thus an ideal introduction to traditional Korea, and whets the appetite for more adventurous forays into the interior - though nowhere does the old way of life survive in quite the pristine way it is presented here.

Before or after seeing the village, it's worth spending some time in **Suwon** itself. Near the end of the eighteenth century King Chongjo resolved to move his capital from Seoul to this city, and in preparation he ordered a great fortress, the "Flower Fortress," built here and the city to be enclosed by massive walls. This was all done according to his will but somehow he never got around to making the move, and during the Korean War the whole lot was destroyed. In 1975, however, the government decided to rebuild it ac-

cording to the original design. Four and a half years and $3.3 billion dollars later the project was completed. The walls, five and a half kilometers (nearly three and a half miles) in length, and the fortress may be freely inspected.

King Chongjo was a scholar and aesthete as well as a builder, and if you stroll up to the North Gate you can catch one of his happiest effects. Just below a pretty octagonal pavilion is an exquisitely landscaped pond. The king apparently liked to relax in the pavilion with the ladies of the court and enjoy watching the reflection of the moon crossing the pond's surface.

Suwon is easily reached from Seoul. Take the subway from City Hall - make sure you catch the right one, with Suwon in *han'gul* on the front - and it will take you all the way, mostly overground. Tickets to the Folk Village can be bought near Suwon Station. On leaving the station cross the road in front of you by the underpass. On the left hand side and a few doors up is the office of the Folk Village, framed by two totem poles. A ticket to the village costs ₩2,500, which includes the cost

ABOVE Aristocratically costumed attendants LEFT and rice-pounding farmer RIGHT at Suwon's Korean Folk Village.

of the bus there and back. Buses leave for the village from right outside the office.

P'ANMUNJOM: WINDOW TO THE NORTH

P'anmunjom is the only place where North and South Korea meet. Here, on the site of a farming village destroyed in the civil war, in a blue-painted hut built of breeze blocks with a corrugated iron roof which straddles the military demarcation line (DMZ), representatives of the two sides have been eyeballing and stonewalling each other for more than thirty years. In one meeting it is

recorded that the North Koreans referred to the United States as the "US Imperialist Aggressor" more than 300 times.

A trip to P'anmunjom is hardly a barrel of laughs, but it is one that no visitor to the country should miss. The only way to do it is on an official tour, arranged by the Korea Tourist bureau which has an office in the Lotte Hotel. It is necessary to book forty-eight hours in advance, presenting your passport at the same time, and tours are often canceled for "security reasons", so be prepared to try and try again. Tour members are not allowed to wear jeans, sneakers or other sloppy clothes, presumably to avoid handing the North ready-made propaganda about Western decadence. Setting off at 9 am, buses return to central Seoul by about 4 pm.

The trip builds slowly during the thirty-five mile ride from Seoul to the DMZ. Beyond the northern suburbs ordinary countryside surrounds you. Then in the middle of a field is a stalled loco-

Traditional methods of smithying ABOVE and paper-making LEFT demonstrated at Suwon's Folk Village.

motive, stalled for thirty years, with notrack to take it further north. In the old days it used to be possible to ride a train all the way from Pusan to Paris.

There are the memorials - to Filipinos who died in the war, to Korean soldiers who deliberately blew themselves up, the world's only memorial to dead foreign correspondents. There is the **House of Nostalgia**, where Koreans hold memorial services and pray for re-unification. Some ten million Koreans suffered family break-ups because of the war. The House of Nostalgia is as close to the DMZ as ordinary south Korean citizens are allowed to go.

Five hundred meters (546 yards) south of the DMZ, at Camp Kitty Hawk, base camp for the United Nations Command Support Group which patrols the DMZ, an American soldier takes over from the Korean guide. After a briefing in the camp and a lunch of roast beef and mashed potatoes in the NCO Mess, the bus takes you to the heart of the matter, the **Joint Security Area**, where more than 400 official meetings have been held since 1953 - the longest continuing peace talks in history.

Visitors can wander about inside the Military Armistice Commission buildings which straddle the Military Demarcation Line; it is even possible to cross into North Korea (the far side of the conference table), and you may take snaps of the North Korean guards peering in at you through the windows.

Apart from the military, the only people living in the DMZ are the farmers of the South Korean village of Taesong-dong. The lives they lead are tightly circumscribed: they must be back in the village by dusk each day and at home and accounted for by 11 pm. In compensation they are among the wealthiest farmers in the country, owning far more land than the average, and are exempt from income tax and military service.

North Korea has its DMZ village,

too, and a brief bus ride away from the Joint Security Area visitors get a good view of it. It's a much grander-looking affair than Taesong-dong, with many four-story brick houses, but it's a sham, built solely to counter-balance the real village in the south. Some fifteen to twenty workers commute here every day to raise and lower the vast flag and turn the lights in the houses on and off, but no-one lives here. That's one reason why the US troops call it Propaganda Village. The other is that loudspeakers in the village bombard the south with the praises of Kim Il-sung six to twelve hours a day, mostly at night.

There is really nothing to *see* at P'anmunjom, nothing of beauty or antiquity, but it is certainly a gripping trip. It offers a rare opportunity to see through the veil of comfortable illusions behind which we live our lives, to the tense and weird rivalry which is behind it. Here, where irreconcilable enemies sharing the same blood and often the same names spend their days in such close proximity - nearly standing on each others' toes in the Joint Security Area - that you might mistake them for

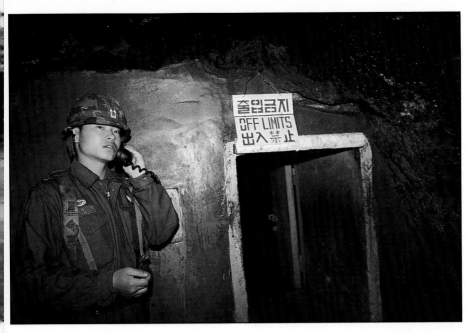

best buddies except that they are armed to the teeth, one gets a vivid sense of the fragility of peace; for if any of these men were to do anything violently unexpected the result could, within days or hours, be the end of life on earth as we know it. This is the reality of the modern world, and it is frequently indistinguishable from the weirdest fantasy. Take the DMZ, for example, which is in fact not demilitarized at all, but one of the most intensively militarized places on earth: despite the million soldiers gathered on either side of it in tense readiness, it has been so uninterruptedly peaceful for more than thirty years that the native bears, wildcats, deer and cranes of Korea have decided that it is the most comfortable place in the country to live. The whole strip has become the peninsula's greatest wildlife sanctuary.

KANGHWA-DO: ISLAND OF EXILE

About 50 km (31 miles) northwest of Seoul, just south of the DMZ and linked to the mainland by bridge, Kanghwa Island has cultural relics spanning Korea's entire history, including prehistoric dolmen, one of the country's oldest temples, and the restored palace of the Yi dynasty king who took refuge there.

Buses leave regularly for Kanghwado (*do* means island) from Seoul's Sinchon Rotary, and the trip takes about one-and-a-half hours.

As you cross Yomha Strait to enter the island you'll notice the remains of walls and fortresses constructed during the mid-thirteenth century. These were built to protect the royal family, who took refuge there during the Mongol invasions. **Kanghwa City** lies just beyond these fortifications.

The town itself is small and rustic, a perfect place for leisurely strolls. Here you'll find some of Korea's best floor mats, doorway screens and rush baskets for sale. The town is also an important silk-weaving center.

Next to the silk factory, hanging in a small pavilion, is a 3,864 kg (8,518 lb) bronze bell cast during the reign of King Sukchong (1674-1720). When

ABOVE and LEFT P'anmunjom's "Tunnels of Aggression", driven four kilometers through solid rock by the North.

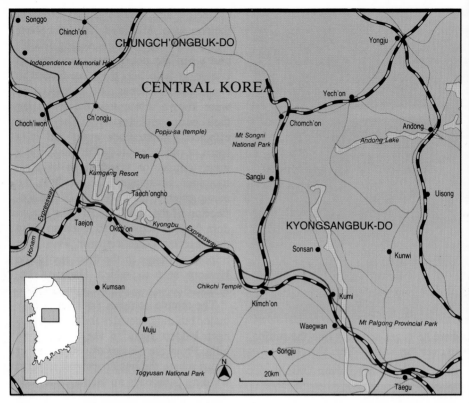

monks and nuns in residence at Haein-sa, about half of them studying the ancient Scriptures stored there, the other half sitting in meditation in the various hermitages. It certainly feels like a very lived-in temple. Peek into the big, earth-floored kitchen and you may see a young monk stoking the fire under the old-fashioned cauldrons with logs. You may also see masons and carpenters at work, for the temple is continuously being restored and renovated using stone and lumber culled from the surrounding mountains.

Up the steep steps behind the main hall is Haein-sa's chief claim to fame: the long, grilled wooden storehouse which contains the tens of thousands of wood blocks on which are inscribed the *Tripitaka Koreana*, the Korean canon of Buddhist scripture.

Commissioned by King Kojong in 1236 while exiled on Kanghwa Island during the Mongol occupation, the pur-pose of the undertaking was to enlist the aid of Buddhist gods in ridding Korea of the Mongols. The text was based on the original and complete Chinese translation of the Buddhist Tripitaka, which was subsequently lost in China. "Tripitaka" means "Three Baskets," these being "sutra," discourse, the Buddha's words; "viyana," discipline, the rules of Buddhist practice; and "apidharma," "analysis," philosophical discussions about the sutra by Buddhist scholars.

The white-birch wood blocks, each measuring twenty-nine inches long, nine-and-a-half inches wide and two-and-a-half inches thick, were imported from China and had to be seasoned for nine years before they could be used. After that, twenty scribes and 180 wood carvers labored for ten years to inscribe the complete Tripitaka on 80,000 of these blocks, with no errors or deletions. Buddhist scholars from other countries still visit the temple to study them.

The library which houses them is the oldest building in the temple and dates from 1488. Two devastating fires which destroyed everything else left the library unscathed, a miracle attributed to divine protection. The library is ingeniously constructed: its altitude is 750 m (2,690 ft), exactly mid-way between sea level and the summit of Mt Gaya. Cold air from the mountain-top and warm air from the valley floor meet at this point, providing an ideal atmosphere for the blocks, and the library is thoroughly ventilated by latticed windows, which ensure optimum circulation of air inside. Elevated shelves and deep troughs protect the collection against flooding. Under the foundations lie thick layers of charcoal, lime and salt, which absorb excess moisture during the humid summers and release it back into the library during the dry winters. The library is, in other words, a masterpiece of air-conditioning technology which requires no moving parts. A few years ago a thoroughly modern library was built nearby, complete with electric fans, automatic vents, dehumidifiers and thermostats - but after a while the monks discovered that the blocks they had experimentally stored there had begun to deteriorate. All were returned to the original library, where they can be expected to survive the next 500 years as immaculately as the first.

Besides the main temple complex there are many other places worth visiting in **Mt Gaya National Park**, where the dense forests, rushing streams and sparkling waterfalls make for exhilarating hiking. Five hundred meters (550 yards) beyond the main temple, for example, you'll find the **Hongje-Am Hermitage**; others nearby include **Geumseon-Am** and **Gugil-Am** both for nuns, and **Bohyeon-Am**. Two kilometers (one and a quarter miles) west of the temple is a tranquil wooded retreat by a cool pool formed by Yongmun water-

fall, while deeper into the hills is a famous seven and a half meter (25 ft) tall image of Buddha carved out of a solid lump of granite, which dates from the eighth century. Those with the stamina might like to hike up to the summit of Mt Gaya and admire the terrific views from the antique Jeonmang-Dae Observatory. **Naghwa Lake**, near the Gilsang-Am Hermitage, is considered to be one of Mt Gaya's "seven scenic sights," while the **Nongsam-Jeong Pavilion**, high up in a grove of pines, stands above a stream bed of spectacular boulders,

over which the mountain waters cascade lustily down to the valleys below.

Winding back down the mountain from Haein-sa - note the umbrella - shaded pit-stops on the way where monks can be observed eating ice creams - you arrive back at the road where the bus dropped you. Ten minutes further on is the little resort village which lives off the tourists visiting the temple. It has over a dozen inns and numerous restaurants and bars, and is the obvious place to spend a night or two if you decide to give Mt Gaya a proper going over. The restaurants here specialize in the wild mushrooms and vegetables which are picked in the mountains, gathered from the surround-

Main hall of Haein-sa Temple: exterior shot.

ing wilderness.

A particularly charming inn here is the **Kook Geh Inn** which overlooks the rest of the village from its vertiginous perch. Built entirely of wood in classical Korean style, it's hard to miss if you walk up through the village.

If you prefer to see Haein-sa and return to the city within one day, it's simply done as the buses are frequent and **Taegu**, much the closest city, has plenty of decent accommodation. Though short on important things to see, Taegu is a prosperous and cheerful place, famous for its apples and its herbal medicine market, one of Korea's biggest.

The apples were introduced during the nineteenth century by an American missionary, James Adams, and are well-known throughout the Far East for their crispness. To see mountains of them visit Taegu's West Gate Market, one of the oldest and most colorful bazaars in Korea. Taegu is the major market center for most of Korea's southern provinces, and the market gives a good idea of the in-

credible volume and variety of produce that pours through the town.

The medicine market, **Yak-chong Kol-mok**, known to foreigners as Medicine Lane, is an equally eye-opening sight, with its herbs and roots, its dried and stretched reptiles and its bundles of insects.

Taegu's increasing affluence is apparent in the many new buildings which line its broad, leafy streets, its massive new churches and the liveliness of the center at night. The area south of Taegu Station (not Dong-Taegu, **East Taegu**, which is where the trains from Seoul stop) is bursting with evidence of prosperity - shop windows crammed full of cakes, vendors' bowls overflowing with strawberries, chic little interior shops selling stripped pine furniture and fancy lamp stands, cafes and night clubs *à la Japonaise*. Standing with your back to the entrance of the Dong-in Hotel, walk down to the right and take the first right turn and you'll find yourself on **Dong Sung Road**, Taegu's "Broadway," its lanes solid with eating and drinking establishments - **makkolli** bars, beer-halls,

Gorgeous interior of Haein-sa Temple's main hall.

restaurants, cafes, salons and clubs. Among Taegu's more improbable temptations is the ornate new French restaurant "**Avignon**," just down the lane from the rear entrance of the Dong-In Hotel, groaning under the weight of its crystal chandeliers, marble trim and rococo detailing. The food is passable.

The other recommended downtown hotel is **Hanil Hotel**, but there are abundant inns - *yogwan* and *yoinsook* - near Taegu Station which offer simple but decent and cheap accommodation.

Places to visit in the Taegu area, besides Haein-sa, include **Apsan Park**, with its cable car running to the peak of Mt Ap for sweeping views over the Taegu plain; **Si-Sung Reservoir** on the southern edge of the city, popular for boating in summer and skating in winter; the Shilla period **Tonghwa Temple**, a thirty-minute drive north of the city, on the steep slopes of Palgong Mountain which offers excellent hiking possibilities; and the pretty little temple called **Yong-yon**, thirty minutes in the opposite direction, which is also set in an area famous for its hiking trails. A little further afield is **Chikchi Temple**, a seven kilometer (four and one third mile) bus or cab ride from the town of Kimchon, halfway between Taegu and Taejon. The temple buildings date back to 1602, though it was founded much earlier. Its most famous abbot was Samyong-Taesu, the high-priest who led an army of warrior-monks against the Japanese during the invasion of 1592-98.

KYONGJU: VALLEY OF THE SHILLA KINGS

Kyongju is one place in Korea where the ancient past starts into life wherever you go. Still perhaps wrestling with the look and feel of the most recent Yi dynasty, still baffled by the different invasions and divisions, the visitor who stays a day or two here soon finds himself enthralled by and overwhelmingly curious about the much older culture of Shilla, of which Kyongju was the heart.

All told the Shilla era lasted nearly a thousand years, from 57 BC to AD 935, and this town, then called Sorabol, was the kingdom's capital throughout. Relics of that long period are richly scattered through the valley. Eclipsed for over a thousand years when succeeding dynasties made their capitals elsewhere, Kyongju's ancient heritage has only recently been re-discovered.

Modern Kyongju is a typical, rather run-down Korean country town, with enough inns, restaurants and bars to keep the visitor amused when he's not exploring the sights but with little of intrinsic interest - though south of the center there are a lot of traditionally roofed houses. Traditional roofs have become a bit of a fad here since the town was identified as one of the country's most important tourist destinations. Even some of the gas stations have them.

The area's real attractions are nearly all well over a thousand years old, and what is amazing is how many there are. Two or three days is long enough to see the most famous and striking places, but those whose curiosity is fired will find it possible to come back time and time again without exhausting Kyongju's possibilities. For such people, *Korea's Kyongju* by Edward Adams (grandson of the man who introduced apples into Taegu) will be helpful. It's full of extraordinary yarns from the Shilla period. The price is ₩10,000 and it's available at Kyongju's National Museum.

Kyongju's ruins are widely scattered, so unless one is traveling in a chauffeur-driven limousine it's wise to plan routes carefully. The following four itineraries require a minimum of taxi and/or bus rides and only a moderate amount of walking.

First Itinerary: Central Kyongju

Tumuli Park: The assembly of gentle green mounds south west of Kyongju Station is the burial ground of King Michu (reigned 262-283) and of at least twenty other Shilla kings. The park was created in 1973 when 180 encroaching dwellings were removed and the whole area enclosed and landscaped. Juniper, pine and bamboo, traditional Korean symbols of longevity, are dotted around the park.

Since its opening in 1973, Tumuli Park has yielded 11,526 priceless relics, which are now on display in the national museums of Kyongju and Seoul. Most of them came from the **Tomb of the Heavenly Horse**, *Cheonma* in Korean, where replicas of some of the precious items found are displayed in wall niches. Visitors are free to enter and inspect although the bones of the king interred here have long since disintegrated, owing to the acidity of the soil, his solid gold crown, his belt of beaten gold, his jade ornaments and other possessions were found intact in their original positions when the tomb was opened.

The crown is without question the

most glorious of these wonderful treasures, and is of a beauty and sophistication that has few parallels in East Asia or indeed anywhere else in the world.

OPPOSITE A section of Pulguk-sa Temple, near Kyongu. TOP Bomun lake resort, near Kyongju. ABOVE Distinctively massive stone frontage of Pulguk-sa Temple, Kyongju.

More than just an extraordinary work or art, it's a dense mass of symbolism. The three tall structures at the front represent cosmic pine trees, the two at the back represent reindeer antlers, and both of these are important symbols of longevity as well as ancient signs of shaman power. The whole crown is covered with comma-shaped pendants of jade, which represent the claws of the tiger, the most potent repeller of evil influences.

The Tomb of the Heavenly Horse is the only one of the twenty burial chambers to have been excavated so far, and

rea under the Shilla banner. The park was originally conceived as a sort of scale model of the united Shilla Kingdom, complete with rivers and mountains, seas and lagoons, pavilions and palaces. It was here in 935 that the last Shilla king finally surrendered to invading forces, bringing the dynasty to an end eight years short of a millennium from its inception. Repaired and restored in 1975, Anapchi Pond is a pleasant park which retains some echoes of its days of glory - though inevitably restoration fell far short of recre-

visitors may feel that the show is a little thin considering the price of admission. Most of Kyongju's other sights are certainly better value - but no other place puts one so thoroughly into the Shilla frame of mind.

A few hundred yards from Tumuli Park to the east is **Anapchi Pond**, the site of royal pleasure pavilions where Shilla kings fished for carp and went boating with concubines, composing verse the while. It was constructed in 674 under the auspices of King Munmu, to celebrate the unification of Ko-

ating the garden as it used to be.

Ten minutes from here on foot is the institution that helps one to make sense of everything else in Kyongju, the **National Museum**. A bold attempt to unite Shilla and modern taste in one design, the museum has a fabulous collection of artifacts from all over the area, including bronze, ceramic, decorated roof-tiles and more of the incredible gold jewelry mentioned above.

In a separate pavilion outside the museum hangs the famous **Emille Bell** (pronounced "emil-leh"), one of the largest and (they say) most resonant bells in Asia. It was cast over a thousand years ago, and a sad story attaches to its creation. It seems that the bellmaker tried over and over again to cast it to the king's specifications, but each time the newly-finished bell was struck it cracked. He was at his wits' end and on the verge of committing suicide when an old monk appeared and told his widowed sister that her brother's task could be accomplished and his life saved only through the sacrifice of her infant daughter. The virtuous sister re-

solved to do her bitter duty, and despite the compassionate bell-maker's entreaties insisted that he do as the monk said. Finally he consented: he carried the hapless baby to his workshop and flung her into the molten metal! When the bell was finally cast, not only did it not crack but its tone was painfully beautiful, reminiscent of a baby's plangent wailing. Hence the bell's name, "emille," which is the old Shilla language's onomatopoeic word for a baby's cry.

This fascinating story combines the ever-popular Confucianist theme of the conflict of duty and human feelings with a human sacrifice motif which harks back to Shilla's much older shamanist tradition. The Shilla kingdom was the last part of the peninsula to accept Buddhism, and shamanist influence was slow to fade.

Visitors unfortunately have little opportunity to corroborate this story, as the bell is rarely if ever rung.

Those with the stamina may finish off this first excursion, after a walk of about twenty-five minutes, with a visit to **Bunhwang sa Pagoda**. This small temple boasts the oldest surviving pagoda in Korea. Built in 634 under the auspices of Shilla's Queen Sondok, the pagoda displays superb relief carvings and guardian statues. Originally nine stories high, the three remaining levels are built entirely of stones cut to the size of, and to resemble, bricks. In the courtyard is a "Fountain of Youth," and whether or not the water adds years to your life, it certainly tastes pure. A 1,300-year-old gilt Buddha graces the main prayer-hall, and the grounds are beautifully landscaped with flowering fruit trees, pine, juniper, bamboo and weeping willow.

Second Excursion: South East

Pulguk-sa and Sokkuram: Sixteen kilometers (10 miles) south east of Kyongju, built on distinctive platforms high on a steep hillside at the end of a long and winding approach road, Pulguk-sa is arguably Korea's most impressive and popular temple complex.

Established in 528 by a minister of the Shilla court, the temple was expanded to its present proportions in 751. There have been twenty-three reconstructions since then, the latest completed in 1973. The present temple is about one-tenth the size of the original complex.

Pulguk-sa is set in a glade of pine and juniper trees. The various halls, pavilions and shrines are located in walled compounds which climb up the hillside, and from the top the temple roofs form a sea of tile. In the main

OPPOSITE Traditional roofs are found everywhere in Kyongju - by government decree. ABOVE Entrance to Flying Horse Tomb in Kyongju's Tumuli Park.

courtyard stand two large pagodas which are considered to be the best surviving examples of Shilla masonry in Korea. The more ornate **Tabotop Pagoda** represents the ascent of man from a base condition to the purity and perfection of Buddhist enlightenment. Opposite stands the strong, masculine **Sokkat'ap Pagoda**, which symbolizes man's descent into the earthly realm. Both are over a thousand years old.

In the main prayer hall sits a large gilt Buddha, and up the steps behind the main hall, in the top corner of the complex, is a delightful small shrine hall dedicated to Kuan Yi, Goddess of Mercy. This hall is a particularly graceful and compact example of traditional Korean temple architecture at its very best.

The Sokkuram Buddha: Up the road from Pulguk-sa, high on a mountain peak which commands panoramic views of the East Sea and the Kyongju Valley, is **Sokkuram**, the "Cave of the Stone Buddha." To get there used to re-

quire a long, hard climb up mountain paths, but today a smooth road winds all the way to the top. Mini-buses from Pulguk-sa leave frequently, and the return fare is included in the cost of admission to Sokkuram. For those to whom the word "pilgrimage" still means something, however, the walk is to be recommended. It puts you in a properly receptive frame of mind for the marvel that awaits you at the top.

From the summit parking lot, a wooded path twists for several hundred meters along the side of the mountain, then takes a final dip and you have arrived. From the lower courtyard with its Fountain of Youth (yes, another one), whose waters are believed to be capable of prolonging one's life by ten years, steep steps climb to the object of the journey, the **Sokkuram grotto**.

The exterior is extraordinary enough; either this building has just been three-quarters buried in a rock-slide, one would guess, or else it is mysteriously emerging from the heart of the mountain. Inside, seated on a lotus dias, is what many who ought to know regard as the most aesthetically perfect, sub-

ABOVE Kyongju coffee shop. Tile roofs and vinyl sleeves against the mesmerizing green of Kyongju's plain. OPPOSITE Honeymoon couple posing at Kyongju's Pulguk-sa Temple.

limely tranquil image of Sakyamuni Buddha ever executed. A marvel of form and proportion, the white granite Buddha faces east toward the East Sea and the rising sun. Even children are awed and silenced by the sight.

The cave-grotto is an elaborate frozen drama on a theme of Buddhist mythology. The entrance hall is guarded by eight fearsome generals in stone relief and two wild-looking guardians in classical martial arts poses. Four Deva Kings protect the inner portal. In a circle around the Buddha are relief images of the Ten Great Disciples and the Eight Great Bodhisattvas.

Due to the large number of visitors, the images are protected behind glass; but the lighting is subtle and nice, and it's arguable that the glass screen only enhances the powerful impression made by the Buddha.

Frequent buses run from Kyongju (passing close to the station) to Pulguk-sa; two of them are numbers 15 and 35. On the left as you approach Pulguk-sa after leaving the main road is Kyongju's **Youth Hostel**, one of the most popular cheap places to stay in the area (it's gigantic), and a little further on is the **Kolon Hotel**, which has a casino. Some of Kyongju's most attractive accommodation, however, is provided in the artificial village at the foot of Pulguk-sa's mountain. The tourist center has numerous shops, cafes and restaurants as well as over a dozen *yogwan*, all designed Shilla style. The price of accommodation is more reasonable than in Lake Pomun's hotels (see below), and the location is ideal for those who would like to take their time exploring the immediate area. Cheaper accommodation, if the price is crucial, is to be found among the *yogwan* and *yoinsook* in the back-streets of Kyongju itself.

A side-trip from Pulguk-sa takes you back down to the main road and then left (south-east) for another four kilometers (two and a half miles) to **Kwaenung Tomb**. Far less frequented than Pulguk-sa, the tomb's mound is entirely encircled by beautifully carved stone reliefs depicting the twelve animals of the Oriental zodiac. What makes this site even more worthwhile are the rows of stone statues which guard the approach to the tomb. Soldiers, civil officials and lions stand in perpetual protective vigil before the tomb of their royal master. The wavy hair, heavy beards and prominent noses of the military figures were probably inspired by the Persian mercenaries who are known to have served at the Shilla court.

Third Excursion: South
Onung Tombs: To the south of the town lie five of Shilla's most ancient tombs, including the tomb of the king who founded the dynasty. There are also several shrines erected here in honor of the founding king, who is said to have been born here from a golden egg left by a horse which flew down from heaven with it. Hidden in a clump of pine and bamboo is another shrine dedicated to Shilla's first queen, who was born, the story goes, from the rib of a dragon.

A fair hike down the main road brings you to **Posokdong Bower**, once the site of an elaborate Shilla pleasure palace. All that remains today is a granite trough shaped somewhat like an abalone (*posok* in Korean). Set in a shady glade, this trough used to be the focus of drunken royal revelries. The king with his entourage of courtiers and concubines would sit around the stone trough while dancers performed for them. Without warning the king would deliver a spontaneous line of poetry, and command one of the courtiers to come up with an appropriate line to match it. At the same time he would set a large bowl of wine afloat in the trough, and if the courtier had not managed to think of something suitable by the time the bowl reached him, he was obliged to drink it down in one. And so it continued, with predictable results - though one one day in 927 the game went seriously awry when it was interrupted by a band of rebels, who retreated only after slaying the king and sacking his palace.

Another good walk away, due south

this time, in a grove of pine trees on a hillside, stand the three mysterious images known as the **Triple Buddhas**. First discovered lying askew on the slopes of nearby Namsan in 1923, these statues display none of the stylistic characteristics of classical Shilla statuary, but rather reflect the massive proportions and bold lines of the northern Koguryo style. No-one knows how they got to the Kyongju Valley. Today they are kept in a walled grotto and looked after by a family who maintain a small shrine in their honor.

Fourth Excursion: Lake Bomun
The attractions of Kyongju are almost exclusively ancient ruins - but not quite. There is one exception. If you are traveling with children and they are gradually becoming cheesed off - or if you yourself could do with a change of mood - head for the new Lake Bomun resort center, a few kilometers due east of the city.

The center is an ambitious project: if the Korean government's plan is realized, Kyongju will before long become a major international resort, as well as a "museum without walls." Currently there are four deluxe hotels by the shores of the artificial lake, with ten more planned, and a children's amusement park on the far side. The lakeside grounds are pleasantly landscaped, and there are big swan boats to take visitors for rides across the lake.

The four day-trips outlined above will give the visitor a good feeling for what Kyongju is all about. Other sites which will repay the small trouble involved in getting there include the following:

Tomb of General Kim Yu-shin
North west of the city center is the tomb of one of Korea's outstanding military heroes. Along with King Muyol, whose armies he led during Shilla's

seventh century campaigns to unify Korea's "Three Kingdoms," he is regarded as one of the "Three Unifiers," the veritable founding fathers, of the Korean nation. General Kim also led Korea's united forces in repulsing a bid by the armies of T'ang China to conquer the emerging Korean nation.

Though smaller than King Muyol's tomb (see below), the tomb of General Kim displays a far greater sophistication of design. Encircled by superbly carved figures from the Oriental zodiac, the tomb lies on a wooded bluff overlooking the Kyongju Valley.

Tomb of King Muyol: Southwest of the general's tomb (too far to walk) is a spectacular group of tombs collectively referred to as King Muyol's Tomb. This king, famous for having conquered the Paekche Kingdom and thus paved the way for the unification of the country, is honored by an impressive monument just inside the gate: on a large stone tortoise sits a heavy capstone writhing with intricately carved dragons, the symbol of his royal power. If you follow the path beyond the wooded area around the tomb, you will find splendid views of four more burial mounds standing against a background of open sky and rolling hills. This site also commands a distant view of the city.

Travelers with sufficient time and enthusiasm may like to venture even further off the beaten track to visit **Pagoda Valley, Buddha Valley, T'ap Valley, Kuksa Valley**, or the more remote **Sungbang Valley**, all of which are well within driving distance of Kyongju proper. Not a year goes by without important new discoveries being unearthed in Kyongju, and every holiday in Korea should include a few days here.

Discovering Kyongju is pleasant all the year round, but the best time to go is in autumn. The annual Shilla Cultural Festival is held from 8-10 October, and then the whole valley echoes with the sound of Buddhist rites, farmers' bands, and noisy parades, and the city famous for artists and warriors who are a thousand and more years underground, comes suddenly and vigorously to life.

How To Get There

To get to Kyongju from Seoul you have three choices of transport: you can take the fifty-five minute flight to Taegu, then transfer to a bus for the hour-long ride to Kyongju; take the *saemaul* super-express train from Seoul Station for a pleasant four-and-a-half hour ride through the countryside (only two expresses a day, though); or grab an express bus from Seoul's Kangnam Expressway Bus Terminal, where buses leave for Kyongju every hour between 7 am and 6 pm, covering the distance along the Seoul-Pusan expressway in four-and-a-half hours. If money is no object you might rent a car and drive there, which would solve the problem of how to see all the city's far-flung relics in a limited amount of time.

From Pusan, Kyongju-bound express buses leave every half hour between 7 am and 7:30 pm from the city's Express Bus Terminal, and the ride takes 1 hour 40 minutes. A shuttle bus also runs regularly between Pusan's Kimhae Airport and the Lake Bomun resort. The most interesting way to travel between Kyongju and Pusan in either direction is by chugging steam locomotive, a recently revived service which departs from Pusan daily at 9:30 am and returns daily from Kyongju at 1:10 pm. The three-hour ride costs about ₩2,000. While the engine is a genuine antique steam locomotive complete with billowing black smoke and screeching whistle, the cars have been comfortably refurbished.

If you prefer to see Kyongju with a tour rather than on your own, but have failed to arrange it beforehand, no cause to worry: there is a wide range of day-tours available in Kyongju for "FIT"s (foreign individual travelers). The simplest is a one-and-a-half hour tour of Pulguk-sa and Sokkuram Grotto; the most complicated is a full-day tour of fifteen major sites. For details, contact the information desk of any deluxe hotel, or Kyongju's tourist information center, located right outside the train station (tel: 2-3937).

PUSAN: SECOND CITY

The republic's second largest city and principal seaport, Pusan is a place many visitors will have cause to pass through on business or en route to somewhere else, but its intrinsic attractions are rather scanty. Located on the southeast corner of the peninsula, and enjoying Korea's mildest weather, Pusan was the only city which the Communist forces failed to reach on their initial thrust southward in the civil war. Some four million refugees poured into the city, however, settling on the slopes of its many hills, and thirty years later Pusan still retains something of the roughness

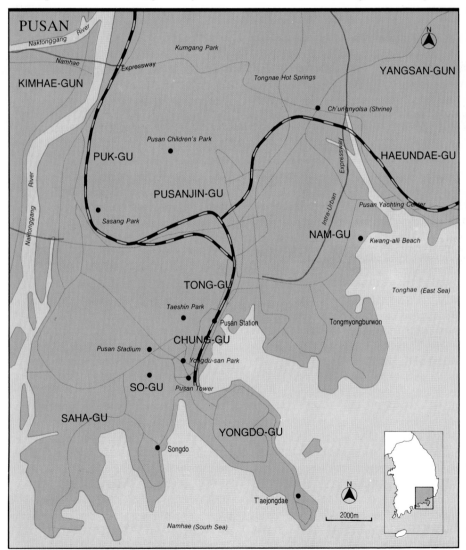

and desperation of a refugee camp. Or perhaps it's the roughness and desperation of a major port. Or a bit of both. Whichever the case, Pusan is the only city in the country where the visitor should be on the lookout for thieves, pimps and other miscellaneous ne'er-do-wells. Many are the innocent Japanese tourists who have arrived in Pusan by ferry from the Japanese port of Shimonoseki and found themselves taken for long and expensive rides by apparently friendly natives anxious to "practice their Japanese." English speakers may be no less at risk.

Pusan's mountainous setting is dramatic, but with its population of more than three million densely packed for mile after mile, it will continue to be a difficult city to get around in until the subway to the center, presently under construction, is completed.

Central Pusan, where the hotels, banks, central post office and train station are concentrated, is the long, narrow strip that fronts the central harbor, with bus terminals at the northern extreme, the train station near the middle and restaurants, bars and night clubs clustered at the south end. If you arrive on the city's outskirts, the first thing to do is hail a cab and head for this part of town.

It's here, too, that the city sights are to be found. **Pusan Tower**, a tall TV transmission tower in the middle of a pleasant park called **Yongdu-san** ("Dragon Head Mountain"), at the southern end of the central strip, has an observation deck which commands fabulous views of the city and harbor. A little farther north is the one structure in the city which deserves greater fame: the **Commodore Hotel**, sixteen stories of outrageous Yi dynasty kitsch, with up-curving tiled roofs, red lacquered columns, fake wooden bracketing, a massive chandelier made out of lanterns in the lobby and, outside the entrance, a whopping temple bell and hammer (ring for service?) The second floor coffee shop does a passable

though expensive pizza pie, recommended for homesick connoisseurs of incongruity.

The **fish market** by the harbor is quite a spectacle, and people who take delight in all the comings and goings of a great harbor, the churning of engines and blasting of sirens and smells of seaweed and diesel fumes, will find their time in Pusan flies by. In the evenings the monied may head for the restaurant zone behind Pusan Tower to eat and drink, while those on a budget or intent on sampling the low life will prefer "**Texas Street**,"

the section of bars, discos and hostess clubs, Pusan's answer to Seoul's It-'aewon, which is one street back from the main road and close to **Pusan Station**.

Hot Springs and Beach Resorts

As well as being Korea's major seaport, Pusan is also one of the south coast's most popular beach resorts. While visitors who want to enjoy the best that Korea has to offer would be wise to do their swimming in, say, the resorts of Cheju Island (see below), if you have to be in Pusan for some time, a trip to one of the nearby resorts is certainly an option to consider.

Closest to hand, not far from City Hall and Yongdu-san Park, is **Songdo Beach**, an inexpensive but often crowded local resort. There are no international hotels here, but plenty of inns and restaurants. The beach itself is pleasant and clean, but the water lies a bit too close to the murk of the harbor for comfort.

Haeundae, Pusan's most agreeable

and up-market beach resort, is eleven miles northeast of the city. Haeundae has several modern hotels, including the deluxe **Chosun Beach Hotel**, said to be one of the best in Korea. A bustling little resort town provides all the facilities of an international resort, and the water is fine. There are hot springs and therapeutic bath-houses in the vicinity as well.

Nine miles north of downtown Pusan is the region's oldest mineral spa, the **Tongnae Hot Springs**, known for its medicinal waters since the late-seventeenth century. There are two tourist hotels and several inns nearby. All have mineral baths fed by natural hot springs.

A little to the north of Tongnae is **Kumgang Park**, a region of dense forests, beautiful mountains and curious rock formations. Numerous historical relics are to be found here, including a fortress tower, a pagoda and several temples. A cable-car carries visitors up to the fortress ruins. There is also an amusement park with various carnival rides for children. Kumgang is known as a good place to admire the cherry blossoms in spring.

Side Trips
Two very worthwhile temples are located within easy striking distance of Pusan. **Pomo Temple**, head quarters of the Dyana Sect and founded in 678, is a few kilometers north of Tongnae Hot Springs (see above), on the eastern slopes of Mt Kumjong. The temple grounds are beautifully landscaped and dotted with Shilla-era pagodas and stone lanterns.

A little further afield is the **Tongdo Temple**, which is rarely seen by foreign visitors even though it is the nation's largest and one of its most impressive temples. It is located halfway

The seafront TOP and nearby seafood restaurants BELOW at Haeundae Beach in Pusan. OPPOSITE Early morning at Pusan's Songdo beach.

between Pusan and Kyongju along the Seoul-Pusan expressway, and has its own clearly marked exit. The final approach skirts the banks of mountain streams by groves of twisted pine and gnarled juniper. Tongdo-sa has a total of sixty-five structures, and almost every deity in the Buddhist pantheon has its shrine here. The temple was founded in 646 by a monk-scholar on his return from studying the Scripture of China.

Pusan is also an important launching point for side-trips to other destinations by boat. Ferries run regularly from a terminal located behind City Hall. There are two entrances: the one marked "tourist" provides a fast hydrofoil service with reserved seats; the one marked

"common" has a slower service, and it's every man for himself when it comes to securing a seat.

The most popular destination by boat from Pusan is the beautiful Hallyo Waterway, two to three hours southwest of Pusan. Hydrofoils leave for Ch'ungmu six times and Yosu three times a day, with stops at Song'po, Samch'onp'o and Namhae. The trip from Pusan all the way to Yosu takes three-and-a-half hours one way. The slow boat sails once a day with stops at the same places, and takes a little over four hours.

Those wishing to drive in Cheju Island may take their cars over on the car ferry which sails from Pusan every day except Saturdays. And if your next destination after Korea is Japan, the Pukwan Ferry provides a service from Pusan to Shimonoseki. This is much the cheapest way of traveling between the two countries. Like the Cheju service, this ferry also sails every day but Saturday.

If you plan to tour the south coast, specially the Hallyo Waterway, the hydrofoil from Pusan is the pleasantest way to get there. The ride takes you through some of the most beautiful coastal waterways in Asia, with hundreds of green islands formed by the peaks of submerged mountains, and timeless scenes of Korean coastal life. The most popular destination in the Hallyo Waterway is Ch'ungmu, a charming town with a very pleasant tourist hotel, from where you can make further side-trips into the waterway.

Both Cheju Island and the Hallyo Waterway are covered in separate sections, below.

CHEJU-DO: KOREA'S MAGIC ISLAND

In China and Korea there have always been legends telling of an island in the eastern sea where the herb of immortality grows and the people live forever in peace and comfort. Some historians have singled out Taiwan as the magic place, but it could just as well be Cheju Island.

Warm and sunny for much of the year, almost untainted by industry, the roads bordered by carefully-tended

131

flowers, full of curious places to go and things to look at and with a relaxed and outgoing population, Cheju is the outstanding place in Korea for a holiday. More and more people are learning about it, but Cheju has by no means been swamped or spoiled, and the people are as honest and dignified as in the rest of the country.

Located 90 km (56 miles) off the southern coast of the peninsula, and shaped roughly like an egg, Cheju is Korea's largest island, and the republic's only island-province. It is 71 km (44 miles) long and 41 km (25 miles) wide and has a permanent population of about half a million. Volcanic in composition, the island is dominated by the 1,950 m (6,400 ft) lava cone of Mt Halla, the highest peak in South Korea.

Cheju is distinctively different from the mainland. The island's shamanist past is still very evident, with stone altars for performing *kut* (shaman ceremonies) maintained in most villages, and phallic fertility symbols, in the

form of the pop-eyed grandfather images called *Harubang*, made of soapstone, scattered everywhere. Shaman mediums regularly perform seances to exorcise evil spirits, invoke the aid of the gods of fertility or contact the souls of the departed. Cheju is exotic, if that word still possesses any meaning.

The popularity of shamanism in Cheju is related to another distinctive feature of the island: its traditionally matriarchal society. In Cheju it has long been the custom for the men to stay at home and take care of the house while the women go out to work. This in turn is connected with the fact that one of the main sources of wealth and subsistence on Cheju is the sea-bed, and as in Japan and elsewhere it is the women who, for sound physical reasons, have always culled it. The *haenya*, the women divers, are one of the island's enduring attractions, and there are said to be still some 20,000 in business, far more than anywhere else in East Asia (though most of them are part-timers). Ranging in age from ten to sixty, these tough women plunge to depths of 15 to 20 m (45 to 60 ft) and stay under for

ABOVE LEFT Young visitors to Pusan's Tong-myong Burwon Temple. ABOVE RIGHT Food stalls at Pusan's Kukche market.

three to five minutes without the aid of breathing equipment.

Cheju's economy is different from the mainland's in other ways, too. With its relatively mild, almost subtropical climate, the island has become Korea's citrus center, producing oranges, tangerines, grapefruit and pineapples for both domestic and export markets, as well as the "Cheju orange," a hybrid of local and imported species. Cheju's most conspicuous crop is rape (mustard seed), and in spring acre on acre of farmland is vivid with its bright yellow blossom.

Cheju is also Korea's most important region for raising livestock. Much of the country's beef comes from the island, and of the country's 25,000 horses, 17,000 are reared here. At the Isidore Ranch, sheep imported from Japan and New Zealand in the mid-1960s produce enough wool to sustain a thriving cottage industry known as Hallim Handweavers, as well as lamb and mutton for the meat markets.

Until about the year 1000 the island remained aloof from and uninfluenced by events in mainland Korea. During the Koryo dynasty it was given the Korean name "Cheju," which simply means "the district over there." Prior to that its local name had been "Tamna." For centuries the Korean court used Cheju as an island of exile, banishing disgraced officials and criminals to its remote shores, much as the Chinese court used Hainan Island and the Japanese, Sado. Due to this fact, most Koreans regarded the island with a mixture of fear and disdain, if indeed they had heard of it at all.

During the thirteenth century, Cheju was overrun by the Mongols, who brought horses and cattle, raising the former for warfare and the latter for food, and leaving both behind when they were expelled from Korea. The animals thrived in the island's lush pastureland and soon became Cheju's ma-

jor industry.

Cheju was the first place in Korea visited by Westerners, albeit accidentally. On 16 August 1653 the Dutch ship *Sparrow Hawk,* en route from the Dutch enclave in Taiwan to Nagasaki in Japan, ran into a severe typhoon in the straits of Korea and was shipwrecked on the shores of Cheju. The survivors were held there for thirteen years. After their escape to Japan and eventual return to Europe, one of them, Henrik Hammel, wrote a lengthy account of their captivity which was pub-

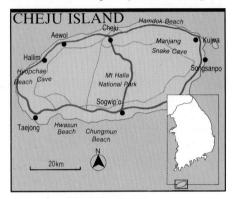

lished as *The Dutch Come to Korea.* It was the first account of the Hermit Kingdom to appear in the West.

Cheju's role in Korean affairs continued to be peripheral until the mid-1960s, when President Park visited the island and took a personal interest in its development. Since then, Cheju's tourist and industrial infrastructure, and its economic importance to the nation in general, have grown rapidly.

Not only is Cheju one of Korea's biggest tourist resorts, it is also the favorite honeymoon destination for Korean newlyweds. Between thirty-five and forty per cent of all visitors to the island are honeymooners and everywhere you go you'll see them, dressed to the nines and usually accompanied by the taxi driver who doubles as official photographer. Sportsmen come to Cheju to hunt pheasant, deer and wild boar in the mountain game reserves, or

to go deep-sea fishing off shore. Others come to loll and swim on the island's dozen beaches, or to hike and camp in the mountains.

CHEJU CITY AND THE NORTHERN SHORE

The island's capital is **Cheju City**, located midway along the northern shore, a town of modest size where the island's mythical founding gods, Ko, Pu and Liang, are believed to have popped out of three holes in the rock. The city has everything the visitor might require in the way of deluxe hotels, restaurants, shops and so on, but most people will probably choose to keep their stay here short. The whole point of Cheju is not its cities but its nature, its mountains, beaches, rocks and flowers, and an overnight stay in the city will normally give enough time to sample the sights and decide where to go next.

For those staying in the city on a budget, the road between the ferry terminal and the market, called **Sanji Ro**, is the place to head for. Many of the city's numerous *yogwan* and *yoinsook* are to be found in the lanes behind this road, and there are also plenty of cheap restaurants here. The bus station is a good hike inland, and the simplest way to get there is by taxi.

Of the things to do in the city, the recently-opened **Cheju Folkcraft and Natural History Museum** can be highly recommended. It gives a useful and attractively designed picture of life in the island, both human and otherwise. The spot where the gods emerged is close by, called **Samsonghyol** ("Cave of the Three Spirits"), and is marked by a shrine.

On the north-western outskirts of town is one of the island's most popular sights, **Yong Du** ("Dragon Head") Rock, an outcrop of basalt formed when molten lava from Mt Halla flowed into the sea and hardened. The local explanation recalls the popular idea that Cheju was the abode of the immortals: according to this, the Dragon King sent a messenger to Mt Halla, the island's tallest mountain, to obtain the secret Elixir of Immortality from the mountain god. Angered by the intrusion, the latter shot the messenger with an arrow, petrifying him in place by the sea shore.

There are four good swimming beaches along the northern shore. **Samyong Beach**, a ten-minute drive east of the town, and **Hamdok Beach**,

fifteen minutes further east are the most popular and have adequate inns and restaurants. **Kimnyong, Sehwari** and **Kwakji** are smaller, less crowded beaches.

On the north-east corner of the island is one of Cheju's geological wonders, the **Manjang Snake Cave** which, at nearly seven kilometers (four and a third miles), is the longest known lava tube in the world. Three meters at its narrowest and twenty at its broadest, the interior is lit with floodlights and may be explored for about one kilometer (two thirds of a mile) of its length. It's chilly and wet so take a sweater and waterproof shoes. Prior to the seventeenth century, a young female virgin was sacrificed at the entrance of the cave every year to appease the Snake

OPPOSITE Special day for a small resident of Cheju-do. ABOVE High school boys on Cheju in military cadet outfits.

is **Chungmun Beach**, one of the island's best, just inland of which is the **Hyatt Regency Hotel**, possibly the only place in Cheju where you can have warm croissants for breakfast. Nearby is yet another waterfall, **Chunje-yon**, with a clear, cool pool at the bottom where fairies are said to play. Here also is a memorial in honor of the shipwrecked Dutchmen who were the first Westerners to reach the island. West of Chungmun Beach is another fine bathing area, **Hwasom Beach**, and west of that is **Sambanggul Temple**, an ancient cave hermitage with a handsome seated Buddha.

The Hyatt is a just a foretaste of Chungmun's future, for an extensive resort complex is planned for this area. It will ultimately include ten tourist hotels, six Korean inns, three motels, 130 private villas and three shopping centers, as well as restaurants, bars, cafes, a marina for boating and fishing and other recreational facilities. As a result, Chungmun is bound to lose what little local flavor it now retains, but as long as little Sogwip'o a couple of miles down the road remains largely

unchanged, visitors will have no good reason to give up on Cheju.

THE WEST COAST

Coming round the great humped bulk

of Mt Sanbang, like the back end of a bison, we swing into Cheju's west coast, where the sea is a lovely turquoise color and, inland, farming couples can be glimpsed shoulder-deep in ripe rice. **Hyopjae Beach** on this side is good for bathing, and close by is **Hyopjaegul Cave**, another well-known lava-tube cavern. But the main attraction on the west coast, one of Cheju's greatest curiosities, is the **Hallim Handweavers' Complex**, in the coastal village of Hallim.

Established more than twenty years ago by Father Patrick McGlinchey, a missionary who has resided in Korea for considerably longer than that, the Hallim Handweavers produce some of the best Irish-style woolens outside of Ireland. The equipment as well as the sheep were brought to the island by Father McGlinchey in the early 1960s, since when the local people have been turning out hand-made sweaters, scarves, caps, mittens and blankets, all in traditional Irish patterns. These rank among Korea's more unlikely souvenirs, and may be bought in Hallim itself or at their special shop in the Chosun Hotel's arcade in Seoul.

Halfway between Hallim and Cheju City you'll find **Hanpaduri**, the remains of a fortress dedicated to the memory of Korea's patriotic *Sambyolch* troops, who refused to capitulate to Mongol suzerainty when the Koryo dynasty surrendered, holding out in this bastion for years before they were finally overwhelmed.

Trekking on Mt Halla

Mt Halla itself is one of the best things on the island, and walking to the top of it one of the "must-dos" for any visitor with a modicum of energy. From where the trail begins on the west side, the walk takes about two-and-a-half hours to the top if you don't stop (which you'll want to) and a little less to get down; from the east side allow about twice as much time. No special equipment is required, only strong shoes or

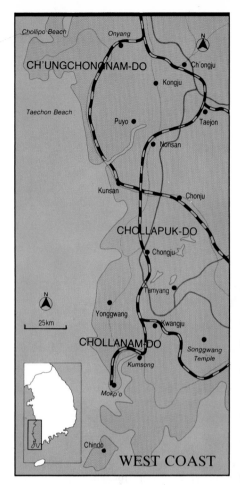

boots and something warm, as it is cold at the peak. Free trail maps are available at the ticket offices at the beginning of the trails (Like most of Cheju's natural attractions, Mt Halla has an admission fee). Be careful to follow the trails sedulously, as it is quite easy to get badly lost on this mountain if you don't.

Hotels and Transportation

Cheju has hotels and inns to fit every pocket and taste, and more are opening every year. While accommodation can be tight during July and August, in the rest of the year there is no shortage of places to stay.

ABOVE Sunrise at Il Chul Bong, "Sunrise Peak," Songsanpo. BELOW Volunteers scything the grass on Mt Halla.

In Cheju City, the best bet for those whose budget will stretch to it is probably the elegant **Cheju Grand Hotel** which is clean and quiet and has an interesting sculpted lava rock garden. More centrally located in Cheju is the **KAL Hotel**, which has smaller rooms and somewhat lower rates than the Grand. The hotel's biggest attraction is its large casino, but during the peak periods, April-May (when the rape flowers are in bloom) and August-October, the hotel tends to become overcrowded with Japanese tour groups.

If you plan to stay in the island for several days and don't want the bother of moving hotels, you could do a lot worse than to make a beeline for Sogwip'o and use that as your base for exploring the rest of the island. With banks, shops and numerous restaurants it is quite as convenient as Cheju and a lot more restful. There are plenty of hotels and inns, too, including the **Prince Hotel**, plonked on a little island just offshore, and **Seogwipo Lions Tourist Hotel**: The pricier hotels such as these cater predominantly for honeymooners - the **Lions Hotel**, for example, has no single rooms - so single travelers may feel more relaxed in one of the town's redoubtable *yogwan*. Several have superb views of the sea. A couple of miles to the west are the Hyatt Regency and other new hotels in the developing Chungmun resort area.

A popular place to spend a night, mentioned above, is **Sunrise Hotel** at the foot of Sunrise Peak in Songsanpo, at the island's eastern extreme. Staying here gives you an even chance of dragging yourself out of bed in time to scale the mountain for the day's big event (sunrise).

As is true in the rest of the country, getting around Cheju by public transport, i.e. buses, is surprisingly and blessedly simple. The only prerequisite is that you know where you want to go; if you can also decipher the destinations in *han'gul* your life will be simpler, but even if you cannot, the local people will always put you right so long as you say where you are aiming for. Buses cross and circle the island with almost incredible frequency, and there is little danger of being stranded even in the quietest hamlet.

The simplest way to get to Cheju from other parts of Korea is by air, and from Seoul, Korean Air operates 106 flights a week with a flight-time of fifty-five minutes. There are also numerous flights from Pusan, Taegu, Kwangju and Yosu. If you are coming from Japan you can fly direct to Cheju from Osaka.

The leisurely way to travel to the island is of course by sea. The car ferry which operates daily between Pusan and Cheju takes eleven-and-a-half hours. Regular passenger ferries ply daily to Cheju from Mokp'o in six hours.

THE HALLYO WATERWAY

The southern seaboard of the peninsula is the location of Korea's beautiful national sea park, the **Hallyo Waterway**. Stretching from Ch'ungmu and Hansan Island in the east to Yosu and Namhae in the west, the waterway is liberally sprinkled with islands, 115 inhabited and 253 uninhabited, which protect the waterway from the rougher seas of the Straits of Korea to the south. This region of unparalleled coastal beauty was declared a national sea park in 1968.

Pusan, far to the east, is the most popular place from which to approach the waterway, and if you are driving, the quickest way to get to it from there is to follow the Pusan-Sunchon Expressway to Masan, then take Route Two south to **Ch'ungmu** in the heart of the park. If you are not driving, the most comfortable and scenic access is by the hydrofoil which runs four times a day between Pusan and Ch'ungmu,

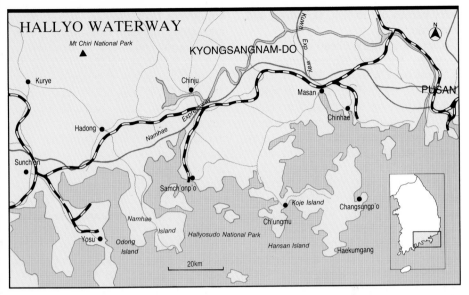

HALLYO WATERWAY

Mt Chiri National Park
KYONGSANGNAM-DO

Kurye

Chinju

Masan

PUSAN

Hadong

Namhae Expressway

Chinhae

Sunch'on

Samch'onp'o

Koje Island

Changsungp'o

Namhae
Island

Ch'ungmu

Yosu
Odong
Island

Hallyosudo National Park

Hansan Island

Haekumgang

20km

covering the distance in one-and-a-half hours. Hydrofoils also connect Pusan and Yosu, as well as other points in the waterway. More details on this hydrofoil service are provided at the end of the chapter on Pusan (above, page 126).

If you are approaching the Hallyo Waterway after a trip down the west side of the peninsula (see Off the Beaten Track for details), start your southern excursion in Kwangju and follow the routes outlined in this chapter in reverse.

The charming coastal town of Ch'ungmu, which has been spared the worst of modern development, should be your principal destination in the Hallyo Waterway. From there you can reach all other places of interest. If you are coming by road from Pusan, you will pass through Chinhae and Masan, two sprawling urban ports with little of interest to the tourist, unless he happens to pass through in spring when Chinghae's cherry blossoms are a pretty sight. The Pusan-Ch'ungmu hydrofoil makes a few stops along the way at towns on the north west coast of Koje Island, the second largest (after Cheju) of Korea's 3,300 coastal islands.

Koje Island is well worth exploring,

but it's a good idea to make it a day trip so you can get back to the comforts of Ch'ungmu by nightfall. The hydrofoil from Pusan will stop at Changsungpo, a tiny town which is the island's main port. From there you may hire private launches to take you around to Haekumgang, an impressive outcrop of sheer cliff which rises straight out of the blue waters of the island's southern shore. Covered with pine and camellia, this rocky bluff is one of Hallyo's "six scenic wonders." It is also a refuge for giant white herons and migrating sea birds from the Southern Pacific. Excursion boats run out to Haekumgang directly from Ch'ungmu.

Ch'ungmu is an enchanting little town which gives one an excellent idea of what life all round Korea's coasts must once have been like. Few buildings are over two stories high, and what evidence there is of the twentieth century is mostly 1950s vintage at the latest. The town is full of cozy little restaurants, second-floor cafés overlooking the streets, beer-halls and local shops. An interesting open market starts at the pier and sprawls for blocks. From the pier, ferries take tourists out sightseeing on nearby islands, and excursion boats

developed and hence attracts more experienced trekkers and climbers, not to mention those who want to get away from the crowds: Outer Sorak can seem a mite too popular when swarming with school-kids and students. Trails here are less well marked than in Outer Sorak, and anyone who fancies tackling them is advised to buy a detailed large scale map of the area before leaving Seoul.

There are a number of ways of approaching Inner Sorak. From the park beyond Sorak-dong you may take the cable car to Kwongumsong and from here trails connect directly to Inner Sorak. Coming from Seoul, the best approach is along the Han River to Inje. From Inje there are two routes into the Sorak range: the northern route, which passes the Chingpuryong and the Misil-

146

from the roadside rest-stop called Chang-sudae Villa, and the **Paekdam Temple**, a considerably longer and more difficult climb along the same trail. Further down the road towards the coast is another trail which leads up to the **Yongdam Waterfall**, the **Pongjong-Am Hermitage** and **Taechong-bong Peak**, at 1,708 meters the highest peak in the Sorak range. Be prepared for an arduous four to six-hour trek up steep, twisting trails if you choose this hike; wear appropriate clothes and boots and bring along water and snacks, for here you will find few signs of civilization. Before reaching Yangyang, where marvelous seafood awaits the deserving hiker, stop off at the **Osaek Yaksu Mineral Springs** for a soothing hot soak.

Sorak is the most scenic mountain park in Korea, and one of the best in the world. A delicate balance has been struck between development and conservation; artificial structures and materials have been kept to a minimum, and all construction is undertaken with taste and consideration for the environment. A five square kilometer (two square mile) park called "Leisure Land East" is currently under construction on a coastal stretch of the park, so let's hope that these standards will be equally evident there, too. Facilities in the park will include camping grounds, hot-spring spas, ski slopes, hunting, fishing, water-skiing, tennis, golf and indoor sports.

The fastest way to Sorak is by plane. The flight from Seoul to Sokch'o takes forty minutes, and the bus-or cab-ride from there to Sorak-dong another half hour. Eighteen buses a day run between Sokch'o and Seoul, and the one-way journey takes five hours. Buses travel to Sokch'o along the Yongdong Expressway to the coast at Kangnung, and this is also the quickest route to follow if you are traveling into the area by car.

ryong Passes and terminates at **Sokch'o**, is the roughest and most remote; the southern route through the Hangyeryong Pass takes you to the coastal town of Yangyang, and this is the most scenic and convenient way to approach the area from inland.

Favorite sights along this southern route to Inner Sorak include the **Taesung Falls,** an easy hike up the trail

LEFT "Snow Peak Mountain" cable car glides through Sorak-san National Park.

The destinations described in **The Broad Highway**, above, are those places which are so special historically, culturally or scenically that they demand to be seen by every visitor to Korea who can possibly spare the time. If you haven't seen Kyongju, for example, a vital wedge of the peninsula's history remains unknown to you; if you haven't traveled around Cheju Island, you've missed one of East Asia's most charming and balmy experiences.

Korea has many other places, however, which, though not unmissable in this way, have a lot to offer the traveler who is in the country for a rather more extended stay. What follows is our selection of the best of these.

AROUND SEOUL

INCH'ON

The traditional entranceway to the country for foreigners, **Inch'on** is Korea's fourth largest city and third busiest port. Long an important conduit for trade with China, it also became host to the first Western diplomatic and trade missions after the signing of the Korean-American Treaty of Amity and Commerce in 1882.

Inch'on earned another paragraph in the history books on September 15, 1950 when it was the site of General Douglas MacArthur's daring pre-dawn amphibious landing, a coup which turned the tide of the Korean War. After twelve days of bloody fighting, this landing led to the recapture of Seoul from Communist forces. In commemoration of the event, a 10 m (33 ft) high statue of the general stands at the peak of Freedom Hill, looking over the Yellow Sea.

Today Inch'on is a busy shipping and industrial town with relatively few historical sites of interest to the tourist. Nearby are the beaches of **Song-do**, which are always crowded during the summer, but if you have time you can take a ferry across to some of the remoter outer islands, or down the west coast, where you will find cleaner, less crowded beaches and pleasant lagoons.

Perhaps Inch'on's greatest attraction is the excellent seafood served in rustic restaurants on some of the nearby land-linked islands such as **Wolmi** and **Sowolmi**.

Inch'on has a major deluxe hotel, the **Olympus**, with 200 rooms, a nightclub, a casino, a large swimming pool and both Korean and Western restaurants. Local inns offer less expensive and more traditional accommodation. If you're traveling by car, the expressway will take you from Seoul to Inch'on in less than thirty minutes.

NORTH AND SOUTH HAN FORTRESSES

There are two major fortresses in the Seoul area which date back two thousand years. **Pukhansansong** (the Northern) and **Namhansansong** (the Southern) were both constructed in the early Paekche period, after which they fell into disuse. Yi kings restored them during the seventeenth century under threat of invasion by the Manchus.

The northern fortress is located to the northeast of Seoul and skirts the ridges of Pukhan (Northern Han) Mountain. With this historic site as a backdrop, the surrounding forests and meadows are popular for hiking and picnics.

Thirty kilometers (18 miles) southeast of Seoul, the walls and seventeen gates of the southern fortress snake for eight kilometers (five miles) along Namhan (Southern Han) Mountain. This impressive fortification, which stands over twenty feet high in places, is the more popular of the two. It was here in 1636 that King Injo finally surrendered to invading Manchu forces. On a clear day the summit provides spectacular views

of the Han River Valley.

The fortress is just east of Songnam. Reach it through Songnam, off the Seoul-Pusan Expressway, or from National Route 3 on the way to Kwangju.

ROYAL TOMBS

Royal burial grounds are among Korea's most tranquil and scenic settings, and there are numerous such parks in the Seoul area. The underground chambers are covered over with round mounds of earth and domed with layers of green turf, marked with simple but elegant stone shrines and set among groves of pine or bamboo.

At **Kumgok**, about forty minutes north east of Seoul by car, lie the **Hong Yurung Tombs**, the graves of Korea's last two kings, Kojong and Sonjong, and their wives. Set in a wooded park full of magpies, orioles and cuckoos, these classical Korean burial mounds are perfect examples of the tranquil, naturally landscaped settings preferred by Korean kings for their resting-places. The white stone guardians, which include representations of war-

riors, scholars and mythical animals from the Oriental zodiac, look like smaller versions of the giant stone statues which keep vigil over the route to the Ming imperial tombs north of Peking.

Near Kumgok is **Tonggu-Rung**, where King T'aejo, founder of the Yi dynasty, was buried in 1408. A little further north at **Kwangnung**, 28 km (17 miles) outside Seoul, is the most delightful of these parks in the Seoul area: the burial ground of King Sejo (died 1468) and his wife Queen Yum Chon-hi. These magnificent mounds lie deep in thick forests, as does **Pongson Temple**, which was recently renovated in traditional style.

More burial parks are to be found just beyond the south-eastern suburbs of Seoul. **Honnhung** contains the tomb of King T'aejong (1367-1422) and Queen Wonkyong, and **Innung** contains the tombs of King Sunjo (1790-1834) and Queen Sunwon. These parks are located in the fertile farmbelt re-

ABOVE Fish dock at Inch'on, the major port west of Seoul which is also Korea's fourth largest city.

151

An interesting side-trip from Soyang Lake entails a fifteen-minute boat ride north from Soyang pavilion and a twenty-minute hike up a steep hillside from the dock. After passing a waterfall, you will stumble upon **Chongp'yong Temple**, a Buddhist retreat founded 1,600 years ago. The temple has especially fine murals on its exterior walls.

Even more remote is the town of **Yanggu**, northeast of Soyang, about a one-and-a-half-hour boat ride from the Soyang Pavilion. The town, accessible from the dock by bus or taxi, is in a secluded valley only a few miles from the DMZ. Yanggu is a typical Korean country town, shut off from most Western influences. There are inns where you can put up if you feel like drinking in the atmosphere at your leisure. Yanggu is as far as you can go in the lake country by boat.

From Yanggu you are within striking distance of **Inje**, inland gateway to Mt Sorak National Park. See **The Broad Highway** for details.

The East Side: Coast Resorts and Mountain Retreats

Stretching 390 km (242 miles) from Hwajinpo Beach just below the DMZ down to the industrial city of P'ohang, Korea's east coast has the country's most spectacular seascapes. A region of many contrasts, the rugged coastline is punctuated by deep ravines and prominent pine bluffs, quiet fishing coves and pretty inland lagoons. The clear blue water and clean white sand make for some of Korea's best swimming beaches. Wooded promontories with old pavilions are found along the entire length of the coast, while only minutes' inland are scenic mountain parks and relaxing hot-spring spas.

To reach the coast from Seoul take the Yongdong Expressway from Seoul to Kangnung. About half an hour before Kangnung on the southern side of the expressway is the **Dragon Valley Ski Resort**, Korea's best, eight kilometers (five miles) from the expressway. The resort has three slopes, all equipped with chair-lifts, equipment rental stores, lights for night skiing and so on.

At Kangnung, terminus of the expressway, turn north on to the coast road and head for **Sokch'o**. This major fishing port has excellent fish restaurants and is only fifteen minutes from Mt Sorak National Park. Just outside the town is the new **Choksan Hot Springs Resort**; to the north is **Hwajinpo Beach**, one of Korea's best beach resorts, where many of Seoul's wealthy maintain villas.

Heading south again, but before Yangyang, is **Naksan Temple**, which dates from 671. A fifteenth century bell and a Koryo dynasty pagoda are among its treasures, but the most famous feature here is the 16 m (52 ft) white granite staue of Kuan Yi, the Goddess of Mercy.

Drive through Yangyang and continue down the coast until you see the sign for **Hajodae Pavilion**. Located on a beautiful pine-covered promontory, the pavilion offers superb views of the eastern coastline. Nearby is **Hajodae Beach**, another good place to stop for a swim.

Continuing south, you'll soon see the sign for **Mt Odae National Park**, pointing inland. The region around 1,563 m (5,128 ft) high Mt Odae is dotted with old hermitages, meditation retreats and Shilla era artifacts. There are also two famous temples, **Woljong-sa** and **Sangwon-sa**.

At Woljong Temple, in the southern part of this mountaiin park, you'll see a fine nine-story pagoda, octagonal in shape, capped by a sculpted lotus and a bronze pinnacle. Woljong's other unusual attraction is a sculpture of a kneeling Buddha, also located in front of the main hall.

Sangwon Temple, situated east of the main peak and higher up than Woljong, boasts the oldest and second largest bell in the country, cast in 725. Like Woljong, this temple was founded by the monk Chajang, during the Shilla era.

Kangnung is a quiet fishing resort which comes to life each spring on the fifth day of the fifth month by the lunar calendar (usually in June) for its week-long **Tano Spring Festival**. The main attraction hereabouts for visitors is the **Kyongp'odae Beach Resort**, a few kilo-

takes about a day, so it's best to set out from Kangnung early in the morning.

Just south of Kangnung is the **Jug-seo-Ru Pavilion**, a thirteenth century pleasure pavilion which was the setting for aristocratic moon-gazing parties.

As soon as you pass the exits for Uljin, look out for the sign to the **Sugryu Limestone Cave**. It's in a park by a reservoir a few kilometers inland, a 470 m (1,542 ft) cave formed over 250 million years ago. Its insides are covered with odd-looking stalactites, stalagmites and other rock formations.

meters to the north, which has inns, hotels and good seafood restaurants as well as a very decent beach.

From Kangnung the drive south used to be quite rough, but recently the whole stretch has been graded and paved and nowadays this section of the coast is reminiscent of California's Highway One between Monterey and Big Sur, with its fabulous shorelines and rugged mountains dropping abruptly to the sea. Allowing plenty of time for leisurely stops along the way, the drive to P'ohang, where the coast road ends,

The juniper tree growing by the cave's entrance is allegedly 1,000 years old, an appropriate sort of age for this favorite symbol of longevity.

Health enthusiasts will enjoy a stop at **Paekam Mineral Springs**, 40 km (25 miles) south of Uljin and 10 km (6 miles) inland. Constructed in traditional style, this large new building houses two enormous bath complexes, one for

---

ABOVE Boy at Popju-sa Temple wearing a chain-link fence and a reminder of the year Koreans cannot allow themselves to forget.

even more remote and quintessentially Korean than Andong, from which it is a half-hour drive to the south-west. The last stretch is slow, winding and bumpy as the road is unpaved.

"Hahoe" means "enfolded by the river," which the village is, and it's this feature, reinforced by the mountains which lie beyond the river, that has allowed the village to survive successive wars and invasions unscathed. The oldest house in Hahoe has been here for more than 530 years; the family of the gentleman who runs the tiny village

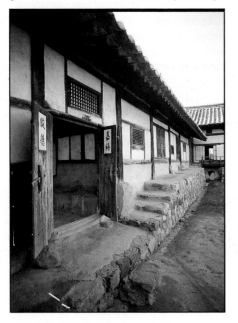

store has lived here for twenty generations, some 600 years. The only modern building is the school, and the government has now come round to the view that Hahoe's archaic appearance deserves to be maintained. All new structures in the village are now being built in the old way, and thatch is used for the roofs, even though it has been eliminated from most parts of the coun-

try in the effort to give Korea a bright modern image.

Hahoe is much like the folk villages of Suwon or Andong, with two important differences: there is nothing artificial about the place, so not only the buildings themselves but also the way they are arranged reflect age-old social realities; and visitors are not so much welcomed as suffered, for the traditions of Hahoe are proud and aristocratic. Use discretion and common sense as you poke around, remembering that people really live here.

PUSOK TEMPLE

Pusok-sa ("Floating Rock Temple") is one of the most inaccessible in the country. Like Hahoe, it is so remote that the Japanese never found it during their sixteenth century rampage through the country. Consequently, Pusok-sa has some of Korea's oldest temple buildings and Buddhist artifacts. About 60 km (37 miles) north of Andong along Route 5, it's a long, bumpy ride along dusty, unpaved roads, but for the intrepid and for students of Buddhism the effort is well rewarded.

The temple was established in 676 by the great Shilla priest Uisang, after his return from China. During his youth, Uisang fell in love with a beautiful girl named Myohwa ("Delicate Flower"), but before he could marry her she was whisked away by court officials and sent as a gift to a T'ang emperor of China. Heart-broken, Uisang entered the priesthood, and ultimately became one of Korea's greatest holy men. During his pilgrimage to China he again crossed paths with Myohwa, whose devotion to him remained so strong that her spirit followed his boat back to Korea and transformed itself into an enormous boulder to protect him and his new temple from the thieves which infested the area. This "floating rock" still balances precariously

convoluted rock formations, is an ancient temple called **Magok-sa,** one of those places that time forgot. The temple was founded in the Shilla period by the aristocratic priest who also founded T'ongdo-sa, Korea's largest temple. The central courtyard has a fine five-story Koryo period pagoda while an 80-foot Bodhi Tree, like the one under which the Buddha attained enlightenment, shades one side of the courtyard.

Fifty kilometers (30 miles) southwest of Kongju along Highway 23 lies **Puyo,** Paekche's second capital. Rich in legends and relics, Puyo is rapidly becoming a major tourist destination. **The Puyo National Museum** houses prehistoric implements found in the area, as well as artifacts from Paekche times.

In a spacious park set on a steep hill in the middle of Puyo is the site where the last king of Paekche made his final stand against invading armies from T'ang China. Among the many pavilions and historical relics preserved in this park, the most dramatic sight is **Falling Flowers Cliff,** a steep and rocky promontory overlooking White Horse River. As the story goes, the Chinese general Su Ting-fang, on the far side of the river, was poised to make his final assault on Paekche when three thousand palace ladies in full regalia hurled themselves en masse from the cliff into the river, preferring death to dishonor at the hands of foreign soldiers. As they fell their colorful skirts billowed out around them. suggesting the image of falling flowers. A pavilion in their honor stands at the top of the cliff.

Facing west in this melancholy park is the **Songwoldae or Moon-gazing Pavilion,** where the last Paekche king kept vigil on the night before his final battle; facing east is the Yongilru or "Sun-greeting" pavilion, where he witnessed what he knew would be his last sunrise. Further down the hill you'll find the **Samching-sa Shrine,** erected in honor of three great Paekche heroes. A colorful ceremony is held at this shrine every October, during the town's annual Paekche Culture Festival.

The town of Puyo itself is pleasant and quiet, with an interesting maze of lanes in the center where markets, restaurants and taverns are located. The place to stay is the relatively new **Puyo Youth Hostel.** Don't be misled by the name, for in addition to dormitory facilities for youngsters, the "hostel" has comfortable private rooms for tourists, a coffee-shop and even a swimming pool. The White Horse River flows a little way down the street from here, while the hilltop park is just behind the hostel.

Southwest of Puyo along Highway 23 is the nondescript town of Nonsan, outside which is **Kwanchog ("Candlelight") Temple** and its far from nondescript **Unjin Miruk, "Buddha of the Future",** the largest stone Buddha in the country. This is something to see, even if it requires a diversion, with its broad and flat but strangely intellectual face and its huge, two-tiered tray-like headdress pressed up against the dense woods behind the temple. Though carved by a relatively unskilled local craftsman a thousand years ago, the image has a rivetingly attractive and mysterious quality. Kwanchog Temple also has a fine five-story pagoda and a large stone lantern, both as old as the statue.

If you can spare a few days to explore the area around Kongju and Puyo, a hike in the mountains of **Kyeryongsan National Park** is highly recommended. Two of the most popular entrances to the park are punctuated by beautiful old temples, Kap-sa and Tonghak-sa respectively, and the steep climb in between, following the prancing course of a mountain stream for

163

and tedious process.

At the foot of Mudong Mountain, which flanks the city, is a new resort with comfortable inns. At the Kwangju Museum are fascinating exhibits of relics recovered from a Chinese ship which sank near here 600 years ago, during China's Yuan dynasty. The displays include some excellent celadon vases and other porcelain ware in perfect condition.

Kwangju is a convenient launching point for tours of the southern coast of the country. For an abbreviated southern tour, proceed east along the expressway from Kwangju directly to Sunchon and head in the direction of Pusan.

CHUNGHAK-DONG

Accessible from the village of Hadong on the Pusan-Sunchon (Namhae) Expressway, Chunghak-dong is one of the handful of villages which have escaped the modernizing zeal of the Saemaul Movement, and here you may encounter Korean life as it was lived centuries ago. It is one Korea's most authentic pockets of classical Confucian culture and society.

Getting to it is rather difficult. From Hadong, about halfway between Kwangju and Pusan, buses depart three times in the morning and twice in the afternoon for the remote village of **Muke**, hidden in a valley on the eastern face of Mt Chiri. The two-hour drive by bus or car is rough and dusty the whole way. From Muke, another two hours of hard hiking will finally bring you to **Chunghak-dong**, nestled in a remote valley 860 m (2,822 ft) above sea level.

As in Hahoe, electricity and television have penetrated to this archaic village, but there is little other evidence of

the twentieth century. Unmarried men still wear their hair down their backs in long single braids, tying it up into traditional top-knots only after marriage. Education is still conducted in the classical Confucian manner by wizened teachers in horse-hair top hats, using Chinese characters in preference to *han'gul* and relying heavily on rote memorization. The clothing, the architecture and the atmosphere of Chunghak-dong are all straight out of a picture-book.

For visitors who wish to stay overnight there is a small *yogwan*, or they may impose on the hospitality of residents. In warm weather, some travelers hike in with their own camping gear, which considerably simplifies things.

CHINJU

Further along the expressway in the direction of Pusan is **Chinju**, a quintessentially Korean town seldom visited by foreigners, where a famous act of patriotic self-sacrifice took place.

Chinju Castle, recently renovated, was the site of two historic battles dur-

---

ABOVE Happy bather in Taejon, a provincial city in the throes of rapid modernization.

166

ing the Imjin War. During the first, the Japanese invaders were repulsed after fierce fighting, but a year later they attacked again, and this time the Korean forces were defeated and Chinju overrun. To celebrate their victory, Japanese officers held a great banquet at Choksongnu Pavilion in Chinju Castle. Among the women brought in to entertain them was the highly accomplished *kisaeng* Chu Non-gae, whose patron, a Korean officer, had been killed defending the town. During the party, Chu Non-gae plied an important Japanese general with wine, then lured him out for a stroll in the moonlight along a cliff overlooking the Nam River. At the edge of a steep precipice she suddenly threw her arms around him, and they toppled together to their deaths. Her patriotic sacrifice is marked every year with a ceremony at the shrine built in her honor above the rock from which she jumped.

MT CHIRI NATIONAL PARK

Northwest of Chinju is **Mt Chiri National Park**. Approaching it from the town of Kurye, you'll come across the **Hwaom Temple**, set in a steep valley which used to form the boundary between the ancient Shilla and Paekche kingdoms. Several national treasures are preserved here, including a four and a half meter (15 ft) stone lantern, the largest of its kind in Korea. The **Kahwangjon**, "Awakening the Emperor Hall", a massive two-story structure with 49 m (160 ft) columns, is dedicated to the Chinese emperor who is said to have funded its construction during the eighth century.

Further into the hills is **Sanggye Temple**, established in 723 by a monk returning from China with the skull of the Zen patriarch Hui-Neng, which he had obta med through bribery. He erected a shrine in Mt Chiri to house his ill-gotten relic, and this developed into the Sanggye Temple.

NAMWON

Some 50 km (31 miles) north-east of Kwangju on the Kwangju-Taegu expressway is the old town of **Namwon**. For Koreans, Namwon is famous on account of the universally-known love story of Ch'unhyang and Myong-nyong, translated into English as *Fragrance of Spring*, which was located here and which has inspired countless Korean books, plays and movies. This is how the story goes:

Myong-nyong the son of a magistrate, fell in love with Ch'unhyang, the daughter of a *kisaeng*. Their romance blossomed and soon they married in secret, for there was no possibility that their parents would endorse such a match. Soon afterwards, Myongnyong's father was transferred to a post in the capital, and the lovers were forced to separate. A corrupt and licentious governor was posted to Namwon, and he resolved to add the beautiful Ch'unhyang to his list of conquests. When she resisted him the enraged governor had her kidnaped, imprisoned and beaten. At this time, however, Myongnyong was appointed Royal Inspector for Cholla Province, and when he heard what had happened to his beloved he rushed to her rescue and severely punished the governor. Bride and groom returned to Seoul, where they lived happily ever after. Ch'unhyang's fidelity is celebrated annually on the eighth day of the fourth lunar month (around mid-March) at a shrine in Namwon erected in her honor.

Chiri itself is a range of stark granite peaks and thickly wooded valleys. Due to the great variety of flowering fruit trees and deciduous foliage, the park is especially enchanting in spring and autumn. It is said that when tea was introduced into Korea from China during the Shilla era, it was first cultivated on

Travelers' Tips

TRANSPORTATION

ARRIVING AND DEPARTING

Korea may be entered from abroad through three international airports: Kimp'o, near Seoul; Kimhae, near Pusan; and Cheju, near Cheju City. All three are modern and well- equipped.

At present fifteen airlines provide regular jet service to and from Korea, with over 200 scheduled flights weekly. Korean Air (KE), United Air Lines (UA) and Northwest Orient (NW) connect Seoul with Los Angeles, New York and Honolulu. The same carriers plus Japan Air Lines (JL) serve Tokyo, while Korean Air and Cathay Pacific are among the airlines that fly from Seoul to Hong Kong, Taipei, Kuala Lumpur and Bangkok. Singapore Airlines (SQ), Thai International (TG), China Airlines (CI) and Malaysia Airlines (MH) are among the other flag-carriers that link Seoul with Taipei and points beyond in Southeast Asia. Paris, Zurich, Frankfurt and Amsterdam are the European capitals served by at least one carrier flying out of Seoul.

Tokyo and Taipei are the two nearest capital cities to Seoul, both a little over two hours' flying-time distant. A stop in Seoul may be included in round-the-world or Northeast Asian tickets at no extra charge.

Below is a list of airline offices in Seoul, both on line and off line carriers. The prefix for Seoul when dialing from elsewhere is 02.

Passenger Airlines Serving Korea:
Air France, Room 218, Chosun Hotel, 87, Sogong-dong. Tel: 753-2574.
Cathay Pacific Airways, Room 701, Kolon Building, 45 Mugyo-dong. Tel: 779-0321/6.
China Airlines, Room 211, Chosun Hotel, 87 Sogong-dong. Tel: 755-1523/5.
Japan Air Lines, Room 101, Paiknam Building, 188-3, 1-ga, Ulchiro. Tel: 757-1711.
KLM Royal Dutch Airlines, Room 110, Chosun Hotel, 87 Sogong-dong. Tel: 753-1093.
Korean Air, KAL Building, 118, 2-ga, Namdaemunno. Tel: 771-66.
Kuwait Airways, Room 236, Chosun Hotel, 87 Sogong-dong. Tel: 753-0041/3.
Lufthansa German Airlines, Room 105, Chosun Hotel, 87 Sogong-dong. Tel: 777-9655/6.
Malaysian Airline System, 14th floor, Dongbang Life Insurance Main Building, 150, 2-ga, T'aep'yongno. Tel: 777-7761/2.
Northwest Orient Airlines, Room 201, Chosun Hotel, 87 Sogong-dong. Tel: 753-6106/9.
United Airways, Room 503, New Korea Building, 19-11, 1-ga, Ulchiro. Tel: 777-2993/7.
Saudia Arabian Airlines, 13th floor, Daeyeonkak Building, 25-5, 1-ga, Ch'ungmuro. Tel: 755-5621/2.
Singapore Airlines, Room 202, Chosun Hotel, 87, Sogong-dong. Tel: 755-1226/8.
Thai Airways International Ltd, Room 208, Chosun Hotel, 87 Sogong-dong. Tel: 779-2621/5.

Airlines With Offices In Seoul But No Direct Flights:
Air India, Room 225, Chosun Hotel, 87 Sogong-dong. Tel: 778-0064.
Alitalia Airlines, Room 111, Chosun Hotel, 87 Sogong-dong. Tel: 779- 1676/8.
American Airlines Inc., Room 103, Chosun Hotel, 87 Sogong-dong. Tel: 778-3351/3.
British Airways, Room 801, Dongmin Building, 95 Mugyo-dong. Tel: 777-6871/5.
British Caledonian Airways, Room 238, Chosun Hotel, 87 Sogong-dong. Tel: 777-8131/3.

Canadian Pacific Airlines, Room105, Chosun Hotel, 87 Sogong-dong. Tel: 753-8271.

Continental Airlines, Room 707, New Korea Building, 192-11, 1-ga, Ulchiro. Tel: 778-0394/5.

Delta Airlines, Room 234, Chosun Hotel, 87 Sogong-dong. Tel: 753-3202.

Eastern Airlines, Room 108, Chosun Hotel, 87 Sogong-dong. Tel: 777- 9786/8.

Egypt Air, Seojin Building, 149-1 P'yong-dong. Tel: 725-1401/5.

El Al Israel Airlines, Room 1302, Samkoo Building, 70, Sogong-dong. Tel: 755-1345.

Gulf Air, Room 111, Chosun Hotel, 87 Sogong-dong. Tel: 779-1676/8.

Philippine Airlines, Seojin Building, 149-1, P'yong-dong. Tel: 725-1401/3.

Qantas Airways Ltd., Room 801, Dongmin Building, 95 Mugyo-dong. Tel: 777-6875.

Republic Airlines, Room 707, New Korea Building, 192-11, 1-ga, Ulchiro. Tel: 755-8945.

Sabena Airlines, Room 707, New Korea Building, 192-11, 1-ga, Ulchiro. Tel: 778-0394.

Scandinavian Airlines System, Room 220, Chosun Hotel, 87 Sogong-dong. Tel: 752-5123/4.

Swiss Air Transport Co. Ltd., Room 205, Chosun Hotel, 87 Sogong-dong. Tel: 777-4864/5.

Varig Brazilian Airlines, Room 505, New Korea Building, 192-11, 1-ga, Ulchiro. Tel: 755-8945.

Western Airlines, Room 707, New Korea Building, 192-11, 1-ga, Ulchiro. Tel: 755-8945.

Airport Tax

All passengers leaving Korea by air are required to pay an airport tax of ₩5,000.

Baggage Allowance

On all flights other than those from the United States and US territories, the baggage allowance is 30 kg (66 lb) for first-class adult passengers and 20 kg (44 lb) for economy-class adults. On all flights from the United States and US territories, passengers are allowed to take two bags, each weighing not more than 35 kg (77 lb).

Transport from Airport to Town

Kimp'o - Downtown Seoul:
Whichever way you go it will take about thirty-five minutes. Exception: the local city bus, which takes about fifty (fare: ₩130), but is available only at domestic airport terminals. Airport bus 601 (₩500), City express bus 63 or 68 (₩350) and local city bus 41 all go to City Hall, near the principal hotels. A taxi will take you there for about ₩2,700, a call taxi for roughly twice that. In fact, nearly all the taxis operating out of Kimp'o are call taxis.
Kimhae to Downtown Pusan:
1 hour by airport bus (₩320), 50 minutes by taxi.
Cheju Airport to Downtown Cheju:
Ten minutes by taxi or hotel bus, 20 minutes. by airport bus (₩200).

DOMESTIC AIR SERVICE

All air services within Korea are handled by Korean Air, which schedules over 100 flights a week between Seoul and Pusan (50 minutes), Cheju (55 minutes), Taegu (50 minutes) and other popular destinations. For information, either visit the head office in Seoul, KAL Building, 118, 2-ga, Namdaemunno, Chung-gu or call (02) 771-66. To make KAL bookings around the country, call the following numbers:
Seoul: (02) 756-2000;
Pusan: (051) 44-0131;
Cheju: (0641) 2-6111;
Kwangju: (062) 232-0551/3;
Taegu: (053) 423-4231;
Yosu: (0662) 62-8123/4;
Sokch'o: (0392) 2-2400;
Chinju: (0591) 53-3906/7;
Ulsan: (0522) 75-8221.
Because of the peninsula's political

Airport and in the lobbies of the Chosun and Lotte hotels. **Cheju Rent Car** in Cheju has 45 cars; check at Cheju Airport. Sample prices:

Pony: ₩26,000 for 12 hours, ₩35,000 for 24 hours.

Rekord Prince: ₩33,000 for 12 hours, ₩47,000 for 24 hours.

Drivers must be over 21 and have a valid passport and international license.

Chauffeur-driven cars: fees include driver, fuel, insurance charge and 10% Value Added Tax. Turnpike and parking fees not included. Sample prices:

Pony: ₩8,200 an hour / 21 km; ₩49,000 a day (6-10 hours / 125 km);

Rekord Prince: ₩11,000 an hour, ₩66,000 a day.

SEOUL'S SUBWAY

Lines 3 and 4 have recently been added to the system, bringing its length to 116.5 kilometers (72 miles) and making it the world's seventh longest subway. Seoul's subway is cheap, fast, clean, safe, and less crowded than Tokyo's (a little). No smoking in the trains, which turn up roughly every five minutes. There are only two fares, ₩200 and ₩300 according to zone.

FERRIES

There are two ways of entering Korea by sea from Japan. The most useful is the **Pukwan Ferry** which plies between Shimonoseki and Pusan every day except Saturdays. Departure time at both ends is 5 pm. The crossing takes seven hours, but disembarking is delayed until morning to allow passengers a full night's rest. Single fares range from US$40 (second class) to US$70 (special first class). Further information: in Seoul, (02) 752-9716, (02) 753-1339; in Pusan, (051) 463-3165/8; in Shimonoseki, (0832) 66-8211; in Tokyo, (03) 567-0974; in Osaka, (06) 345-2245.

costly way to see Korea is by private car, either self- or chauffeur-driven. Five excellent expressways slice through and across the peninsula:

Kyongbu (Seoul-Pusan),

Honam (Taechon-Kwangju),

Yongdong (Suwon-Kangnung),

Namhae (Kwangju-Sunchon-Masan-Pusan) and

'88 Olympic Expressway (Kwangju-Taegu).

These and the ancillary county roads pass through Korea's most scenic mountains, valleys and farm-lands, and they are a pleasure to drive on. The inflated price of gasoline may hurt your pocket but it keeps the roads pleasantly empty.

As yet, Korea's car rental system remains underdeveloped, and Seoul and Cheju are the only places where cars may be rented. **Hertz Korean Rent-a-Car** in Seoul has 320 cars available (tel: (02) 585-0801/5, (02) 798-0801/3, (02) 724-7465), and offices at Kimp'o

ABOVE Cheerful passengers aboard a bus in Seoul: one of the easiest ways to see the city - if you can read Han'gul.

178

The **Kukche Ferry** links Japan's second city, Osaka, with Pusan. The ferry sails twice a week, leaving Osaka at 2 pm on Tuesday and Friday and departing Pusan on Sunday and Wednesday at 6 pm. The crossing takes 21 hours and fares range from $71 to $150. For further details contact (02) 784-3333 in Seoul, (051) 463-7000 in Pusan and (06) 266-1111 in Osaka.

Numerous domestic ferries sail between Korea's coastal towns and offshore islands. The following are the most useful and important:

Pusan-Cheju Car Ferry: Departure (from both ports): 7:30 pm, daily except Sundays. Length of crossing: eleven-and-a-half hours. Fares range from ₩10,780 (third class) to ₩78,040 (special class); price for vehicles ranges from ₩48,400 to ₩21,000. Advance ticket sales:

Seoul: (02) 730-7316;
Pusan: (051) 463-0605;
Cheju: (0641) 2-0291;
Mokp'o: (0631) 2-9391.

Mokp'o-Cheju Car Ferry: Mokp'o

departure 4 pm daily except Sundays; Cheju departure, 7 am daily except Mondays. Length of crossing: five-and-a-half hours. Fares range from ₩7,340 (third class) to ₩57,800 (special class); price for vehicles ranges from ₩41,600 to ₩104,000. Advance ticket sales: as above.

P'ohang-Ullung Island: One round trip a day during summer (May-August). P'ohang departure: 10 pm, Ullung departure 9:30 am. Year-round daily service: departs P'ohang, Ullung 10 am. Length of crossing: 7 hours. Fares range from ₩11,770 (second class) to ₩17,650 (first-class berth). Advance sales:

Seoul: (02) 598-2101;
P'ohang: (0562) 2-0711;
Ullung: 2602.

Pusan-Ch'ungmu-Yosu Hydrofoil: The hydrofoil "Angel" skims the length of the Hallyo Waterway, traveling six

ABOVE Theoretically more convenient than buses, Seoul's taxis can be very troublesome, as some of the faces in this line eloquently suggest.

times a day from Pusan to Ch'ungmu (with stops in Songp'o) and three times daily between Ch'ungmu and Yosu (with stops in Samch'onp'o and Namhae). Length of trip: Pusan-Ch'ungmu: one-and-a-half hours; Ch'ungmu-Yosu: 1 hour and 50 minutes. Sample fares: Pusan-Ch'ungmu, ₩6,250; Pusan-Yosu: ₩12,300. For reservations call:

Seoul (02) 734-5636;
Pusan: (051) 44-3851;
Ch'ungmu: (0557) 2-2091;
Yosu: (0662) 63-2824.

like within the period indicated, as long as they do not work:

Austria: 90 days;
Bangladesh: 90 days;
Belgium: 60 days;
Chile: 90 days;
Colombia: 90 days;
Costa Rica: 90 days;
Denmark: 60 days;
Dominican Rep.: 90 days;
Finland: 60 days;
France: 30 days;
West Germany: 60 days;
Greece: 3 months days;

ENTRY FORMALITIES

Foreigners wishing to enter Korea must have a valid passport or entry permit. Those with confirmed outbound tickets may stay for up to 15 days without a visa. Visitors from the following countries are allowed to stay as long as they

Iceland: 60 days;
Italy: 60 days;
Lesotho: 60 days;
Liberia: 90 days;
Luxemburg: 60 days;
Mexico: 3 months;
Malaysia: 3 months;
Netherlands: 60 days;
Norway: 60 days;
Peru: 90 days;
Portugal: 60 days;
Singapore: 90 days;
Spain: 60 days;
Surinam: 60 days;

ABOVE Building the subway cost Seoul a fortune it does not possess, but it has made life considerably easier for residents.

Sweden: 60 days;
Switzerland: 3 months;
Thailand: 90 days;
Tunisia: 30 days;
Turkey: 60 days;
United Kingdom: 60 days.

Visitors from other countries who plan to stay longer than 15 days can obtain a visa from a Korean Embassy or Consulate before coming to the country. Visas are of two types: up to 90 days, for tourists; and longer than 90 days, for which an entry permit must be obtained from the Ministry of Justice. All who stay longer than 90 days must also apply for a residence certificate at the local District Immigration Ofice. To extend a visa, visit the District Immigration Office at least one day before the visa expires.

These are the addresses and phone numbers of the principle immigration offices:

Immigration Bureau, Ministry of Justice, 2nd Unified Government Building, 1, Chungang-ri, Kwach'on-myon, Shihung-gun, Kyonggi-do. Tel: (02) 503-7096.

Seoul Immigration Office: 39-1, Sosomun-dong, Chung-gu, Seoul. Tel: (02) 776-8984/7.

Kimp'o Immigration Office: Kimp'o International Airport, Seoul. Tel: (02) 662-7611/5.

Pusan Immigration Office, 17-27, 4-ga, Chungang-dong, Chung-gu, Pusan, Tel: (051) 463-7161/5.

Kimhae Immigration Office, Kimhae International Airport, Kyongsangnam-do, Tel: (051) 98-1871/3.

Cheju Immigration Office, 740-3, Konip-dong, Cheju, Cheju Island. Tel: (0641) 2-3494/5.

CUSTOMS

You can bring the following items into Korea without paying duty: two bottles of spirits (up to 760 cc each), 400 cigarettes, 50 cigars, 250 g pipe tobacco, 100 g snuff or other tobacco, or any combination within the limit of 500 g in total. If you bring in books, other printed matter, films, records or anything else that the authorities deem subversive, you're likely to lose them.

EXPORT

There are strict limits on the export of items more than 50 years old, specimens of wildlife (live or stuffed), and ginseng. Get your permit for the export of an tiques from the **Cultural Property**

Preservation Bureau, near Kyongbokkung Palace, Seoul, tel: (02) 725-3053. For five or fewer pieces, permits may also be obtained from the bureau's Kimp'o Airport branch office, tel: (02) 662-0106.

QUARANTINE

Visitors entering from cholera-affected regions should carry a vaccination certificate. Animals and animal products, plants and plant products must all be declared on arrival. Dogs and cats must be accompanied by a veterinarian health certificate issued at point of origin and a rabies vaccination certificate. They are subject to a quarantine period of

ABOVE The cheapest way to enter Korea from abroad is on the Pusan-Shimonoseki ferry from Japan. It sails every day except Saturday, and completes the crossing in seven hours.

ten days

CLIMATE AND CLOTHING

Korea gets it all ways: it's bitter in winter and sticky in summer. In between it has some of the world's nicest weather, and the wheeling of its four distinct seasons is a pleasure in its own right.

Spring: The spring thaw begins in April and the season lasts until mid-June. Average temperatures range between 10-16°C (50-60°F) in Seoul. Spring weather is warm but changeable, with not infrequent showers. Take lightweight clothes for this season, plus a few lightweight sweaters and jackets for cool evenings and chilly mountain air.

Summer: Summer proper is preceded by a month-long rainy season, then from mid-July to mid-September the weather is hot and humid with occasional thunder showers. Temperatures range from 18-24°C (65-75°F) in the north to 24-30°C (75-85°F) in the south. Appropriate summer clothing would include light cotton sports shirts, loose-fitting pants, swimsuits, and some form of light rain gear.

Autumn: The best season to travel through Korea, fall lasts from mid-September to mid-November, as Siberian northerlies re-enact their yearly battle with Pacific southerlies. Average temperatures range between 12-18°C 55-65°F) and the weather is distinguished by long periods of brilliantly clear, dry weather. Lightweight clothes, with sweaters and jackets for evening and mountains, will see you through.

Winter: Lasts from mid-November to March and ranges from cold to bitter. In January and February temperatures are down between -12 to 2°C (10-35°F). Appropriate clothing would include warm woolen pants, heavy shirts, heavy sweaters and jackets, a winter overcoat, and long underwear if you intend to visit any national parks.

CURRENCY

The unit of Korean currency is won (₩). Coin denominations are ₩1, ₩5, ₩10, ₩50, ₩100. Banknotes come in ₩500, ₩1,000, ₩5,000 and ₩10,000 denominations.

The exchange rate fluctuates, but at the time of going to press US$1 = ₩850. Foreign currencies can be converted at banks, hotels and other authorized money-changers around the country. Any amount larger than $5,000 must be declared when entering the country. Unused won may be reconverted into foreign currencies up to a limit of $1,000. You can only take out as much foreign currency as you declared on arrival.

Major credit cards such as American Express, Visa, Master Charge and Diner's Club are accepted at most large hotels, department stores and restaurants in the big cities.

COMMUNICATIONS

MAIL

Seoul's central post office is located on Ch'ungmu Road, a block east of Shinsegye Department Store, just across from the Chinese Embassy. There are convenient branch offices near the intersection of T'aep'yong and Chong Streets, and on Yulkok Street near the Anguk Immigration Office. Stamps are available in most hotels.

Regular stamped letters and postcards may be dropped into any mailbox, but all overseas parcels must be mailed and picked up at the International Post Office across from Yonsei

University in Yonhi-dong. All incoming and outgoing mail in Korea is subject to government inspection. Delivery time to and from Europe and America is 9-14 days, while local mail takes 2-3. Post office hours are 9 am to 5 pm Monday through Friday and 9 am to 1 pm on Saturday.

TELEPHONES

Local calls may be dialed from the red and green public phones found in hotels, public buildings and booths around the country. Two ten-won coins must be inserted after lifting the receiver and before dialing; calls are automatically terminated after three minutes.

Long distance calls within Korea may be made from the large yellow pay phones in hotels, post offices and on the street. Both ten-won and hundred-won coins may be used, and when you hear bleeps it is time to insert more money. Unused coins are automatically returned when you hang up.

Area codes within Korea are as follows:

Seoul 02
Pusan 051
Taegu 053
Inch'on and Puchon 032
Kanghwa 0349
Kimp'o 034
Tongduch'on 0351
Munsan 0348
Songnam 0342
Suwon 0331
Anyang 0343
Yoju 0337
Osan 0339
Yong-in 0335
Uijongbu 0351
Ich'on 0336
Kangnung 0391
Tonghae 0394
Sokch'o 0392
Wonju 0371
Ch'olwon 0353
Ch'unch'on 0361

Samch'ok 039
Ch'ongju 0431
Ch'ungju 0441
Kongju 0416
Taejon 042
Puyo 0463
Onyang 0418
Ch'onan 0417
Kunsan 0654
Namwon 0671
Iri 0653
Chonju 0652
Kwangju 062
Mokp'o 0631
Yosu 0662
Kyongju 0561
Andong 0571
P'ohang 0562
Masan and Ch'angwon 0551
Ulsan 0522
Chinju 0591
Chinhae 0553
Ch'ungmu 0557
Sogwip'o 0642
Cheju 0641

International calls: You can place international calls through the operators at major hotels, or at the International Telecommunications Exchange, on Sejong Road, near the Sejong Cultural Center. Seventy-five countries may be dialed from phones connected to the International Subscriber Dialing (ISD) system by first dialing the international access code (001) then the country and area codes and the individual number. For further details dial 1030. For operator-assisted calls, dial 1035 or 1037 in Seoul and 117 elsewhere.

Telegrams: You may write out telegrams at the International Telecommunications Building on Sejong Road or dictate them over the phone by dialing 115. The former method is surer. "Urgent" telegrams take 6 hours, "Ordinary," 12 hours, and "Letter Telegrams," 24 hours. The International Telecommunications Building is open from 9 am to 5 pm

Monday to Friday and 9 am to 1 pm on Saturday.

RADIO AND TELEVISION

Twiddle the knobs of your hotel radio and you'll find a rich assortment of soap operas, traditional and western music and unfathomable news and discussion programs. Four major radio stations broadcast nationwide, and in addition the **American Forces Korea Network** broadcasts news and music exclusively in English 24 hours a day, with international news reports every hour on the hour.

Likewise the two major Korean TV stations, whose soaps and commercials give wonderful insights into the state of contemporary Korean culture, are usefully augmented by **AFKN-TV** which broadcasts popular American comedy shows, movies and news programs.

NEWSPAPERS, PERIODICALS AND OTHER PUBLICATIONS

Six nationally distributed newspapers are currently published in Korea, in-

cluding one in Chinese and two in English. They appear daily except for Mondays and national holidays. The two English language papers are the *Korea Herald* and the *Korea Times*. Neither is a giant of the newspaper world, and most of their stories are drawn from the wire services. The president is usually on the front page, patting small heads, while riots and other uncongenial domestic matters are relegated to the back. Both papers are available in hotels, kiosks and news stands throughout the country. Other English-language papers available in Korea are the *Asian Wall Street Journal*, the *International Herald Tribune* and the Pacific edition of *Stars and Stripes*, the American military paper.

English language periodicals published in Korea include *Korea Journal* (published by UNESCO), and the weekly *Korea News Review*, a digest of the Korea Herald. *Korea Quarterly* is an English language magazine of Korean culture.

Foreign periodicals available in Korea

ABOVE Buddha's Birthday celebration at Chogye-sa Temple, Seoul's principle Buddhist temple.

184

include *Time, Newsweek* and the *Far East Economic Review*. All foreign publications brought into Korea are subject to government censorship, though this has been gradually relaxed in the past few years.

The best place in Seoul to find English language books, whether on Korean or other subjects, is the bookstore in the basement of the Kyobo Building, opposite Sejong Cultural Center. English language books on Korean subjects are found in the "Government Publications" section.

ACCOMMODATION

For visitors with a modicum of flexibility, accommodation is not a serious problem in Korea. Hotels of international quality are found only in the major cities and resorts, but clean and decent accommodation of a more modest order is found everywhere. The lists of hotels, inns and hostels which follow descriptions of major destinations in **The Broad Highway** will be useful for those who care to book in advance and like to see every step of the way ahead of them. Others may prefer to memorize the han'gul characters for the different species of inn and try their luck on arrival.

YOGWAN

International hotels need no explanation, but the Korean varieties of ordinary hotel, inn and hostel have certain peculiarities.

Essentially, ordinary hotels and inns (*yogwan*, written 여관 in *han'gul*) are distinguished only by the facilities they provide and the rates they charge. In an ordinary hotel, as defined by the authorities, each room has its own bathroom with toilet and running h and c; the room is air-conditioned and furnished Western-style. The *yogwan* is an inn where over one-third of the rooms are equipped with their own bathrooms. You may be provided with a regular western bed or with a Korean *yo* (mattress or *futon*), *ibul* (quilt) and *pyogae* (pillow). There may or may not be some Western furniture; either way the floor will probably be heated by *ondol* (except in summer), and air-conditioning will be in the form of an electric fan. The guest will normally be expected to take his meals in the town, and to pay for the room when checking in. A night at a *yogwan* will cost around ₩10,900; at an ordinary hotel, between ₩12,700 (for a smaller or *Ul* hotel and ₩15,000 (for larger so-called *Kap* hotels).

What the *yogwan* will *not* normally provide is the ambience of Old Korea: the large majority are bald concrete boxes, just like the hotels. The Japanese word *ryokan* and the Korean *yogwan* are written with the same Chinese characters (they mean "travel building"), but equivalents of Japan's elegant traditional *ryokan* are sadly rare; possibly the best in the country is the Un Dang Yogwan described in the **Seoul** section of **The Broad Highway**, above.

YOINSOOK

The one category of accommodation which retains much of the atmosphere of the old days is so humble that the Korea National Tourism Corporation does not even care for foreigners to know about it, yet for seekers of the curious and characteristic as well as travelers on tight budgets, the *yoinsook* demands to be tried.

The *yoinsook* (여인숙 in *han'gul*) is the category of inn below the *yogwan*, and they are found in great quantity in every town and city, usually close to train and bus stations. The building may be a low, traditional one, with a heavy tile roof, and the rooms may open off a courtyard. Facilities are basic: ashtray, towel, tea, bedding which the guest spreads out himself. The communal bathroom is likely to have cold water only and the lavatory may lack plumbing, but in general the standards of cleanliness are decent. Some have improbably archaic views of forgotten corners of the city from their windows; some have caged peacocks at the front gate or guests who sing all night. It's a matter of pot luck. Room rates may be as low as ₩4,000 or as high as ₩8,000 a night, depending on the facilities provided. As with all hotels and inns in the country, rates are fixed by the government and you get as much or as little as you pay for.

Youth hostels are another possibility. At present there are only twenty in the whole country, all located at popular resorts such as Mt Sorak and Kyongju. Besides the familiar dormitory accommodation, most provide double rooms as well. Principle ones are listed in **The Broad Highway** under particular destinations. For information about others, contact the **Korea Youth Hostel Association**, 27-1, Sup'yo-dong, Chung-gu, Seoul. Tel: (02) 66-2896.

TOURIST INFORMATION

Korea attracted 1,093,000 foreign visitors in 1981 and nearly 1,300,000 in 1984, and the number is bound to continue rising during the coming years. Evidence of how seriously the government takes this important source of foreign exchange is seen in the efforts made to enable visitors to enjoy themselves. The Korea National Tourism Corporation (KNTC) has a big headquarters building in Seoul with an excellent new information center in the basement. There are several other infor-

mation centers and counters in Seoul and other cities, and one complaint center. Details are provided below. Besides helping with maps, pamphlets and hotel directories, they also have specialized literature to advise people planning to hold conventions in the country. KNTC is not a travel agent, however. For practical help with reservations and tickets, contact one of the travel agents further down. **KNTC Head Office**: KNTC Building, 10, Ta-dong, Chung-gu, Seoul. Tel: (02) 757-6030

Kimp'o Airport Information Center: 1st floor, Airport Terminal Building., Kimp'o International Airport, Seoul. Tel: (02) 662-2182/3.

Kimhae Airport Information Center: 218, Taejo 2-dong, Puk-gu, Pusan. Tel: (051) 98-1100.

Cheju Airport Information Center: 2096, Yongdam-dong, 3-do, Cheju. Tel: (0641) 7-0528.

Seoul Tourist Information Center: The center (directly behind City Hall. Tel: (02) 731 6337 is open 9 am to 6 pm Monday to Friday, 9 am to 1 pm Saturday. The center also has the following information counters:

Kimp'o International Airport Terminal, tel: 662-9248

Seoul Railway Station, tel: 779-3643

Seoul Express Bus Terminal, tel: 598-4152

Chongno, tel: 734-0023

Kwanghwamun, tel: 734-0027

Myong-dong, tel: 779-3645

Namdaemun, tel: 779-3644

Tongdaemun, tel: 272-0348

If something seems badly wrong, contact **KNTC Tourist Complaint Center** in Seoul, tel: 725-0101. If you want to make a complaint when you are outside Seoul, dial the area code followed by 0101 and you will be put through to the tourist administration section of the local government. Exceptions: **Kyongju**, tel: (0561) 2-8000; **Sokch'o**, tel: (0392) 2-3171/7; **Kyongsangnam-do Prov-**

ince, tel: (0451) 22-1792.

Goodwill Guides Campaign

The run-up to the Olympics will surely show an increase in the number of volunteer "goodwill guides" roaming the streets and helping foreign visitors who are in trouble. They wear badges with smiling faces superimposed on the national yin-yang emblem.

TRAVEL AGENTS

These are the Seoul addresses and phone numbers of some of the major ones:

Aju Tourist Service Co. Ltd., 21-1, Sosomun-dong, Chung-gu. Tel: (03) 753-5051/4.

Chowon Tourist Co. Ltd., 1st and 11th floor, Konpyong Building, 5-1, Konpying-dong, Chongno-gu. Tel: 744-5544/6.

Dong Yang Express Travel Service Inc., 84-18, 5-ga, Namdaemunno, Chung-gu. Tel: 753-0011/4.

Far East Tours Ltd, 4 Floor Namyong Building, 809-16 Yoksam-dong, Kangnam-gu. Tel: 561-0091/5.

Eastwest Travel Service Co. Ltd., Room 802, Koreana Hotel, 61-1, 1-ga, T'aep'yongno, Chung-gu. Tel: 735-8734/8.

Global Tours Ltd., 57-9 Sosomun-dong, Hung-gu. Tel: 777-9921/9.

Hannam Tourist Corp., 89-4, Kyong-un-dong, Chongno-gu. Tel: 313-2131.

Kolon Express Tour Co., 12th floor, Sangyong Building, 24-1, 2-ga, Cho-dong, Chung-gu. Tel: 273-5461/5.

Korea Tourist Bureau Ltd., 728 Soch'o-dong, Kangnam-gu. Tel: 585-1191.

Korea Travel Company Ltd., Room 301, Dongyang Building., 112-6, Sogong-dong, Chung-gu. Tel: 777-0981/5.

Lotte Travel Service Ltd., 27-1, Sup'yo-dong, Chung-gu. Tel: 65-4151/5.

Sam Yong Travel Service Co.Ltd., Room 1003, Songgi Building. Tel: 719-4814/7.

Seoul Orient Express Corp., 5th floor, Kyongwun Building, 70 Kyingun-dong, Chongno-gu. Tel: 732-2628/9.

The Korea Express Travel Service Co. Ltd, 58-12, Sosomun-dong, Chung-gu. Tel: 777-8871/6.

The Korea Times Travel Ltd., 12th floor, Korea Times Building, 14 Chunghak-dong, Chongno-gu. Tel: 734-0071.

ORGANIZED TOURS

Guided tours are operated by two of the agents listed above, Global Tours and Korea Tourist Bureau. These range from morning and afternoon tours of Seoul's palaces and markets to two night/three day tours of Kyongju and Pusan. The only way to see P'anmunjom is on a tour such as this. Contact the agencies for further details. Similar tours are run by some other agencies.

EMBASSIES

Argentina: 793-4062
Australia: 720-6490/5
Austria: 723-7330
Belgium: 793-9611
Bolivia: 742-7170
Brazil: 720-4769
Canada: 776-4062/8
Chile: 792-9519
Republic of China: (Taiwan): 776-2721/5
Colombia: 794-5770
Costa Rica: 725-5877
Denmark: 792-4187/9
Dominican Republic: 792-1850
Ecuador: 792-1278
Finland: 732-6223
France: 362-5547/9
Gabon: 562-9912/3
West Germany: 779-3271/3
Guatemala: 793-1319
Haiti: 797-9372
Holy See: 732-5725
India: 724-4278/9

Indonesia: 782-5116/9
Iran: 793-7751/3
Italy: 722-5980
Japan: 733-4272
Liberia: 793-6704
Libya: 532-0306
Malaysia: 792-9203
Mexico: 741-4060
Netherlands: 793-0651/2
New Zealand: 720-4255
Norway: 792-6850
Oman: 797-8846/7
Pakistan: 313-0427/8
Panama: 720-4164
Paraguay: 794-5553
Peru: 792-2235
Philippines: 720-4860
Saudi Arabia: 313-0631/5
Spain: 720-4564
Sweden: 720-4767
Switzerland: 744-9511/4
Thailand: 792-3098
Turkey: 794-0255
United Kingdom: 725-7341/3
United States: 732-2601/19
Uruguay: 798-0561
Venezuela: 741-0036/7

SELECTED KOREAN EMBASSIES ABROAD

Australia (Canberra): tel: 733044
Belgium (Brussels): tel: (02) 375-3980
Canada (Ontario): tel: (613) 232-1715
Republic of China (Taipei): tel: 761-9363
Denmark (Copenhagen): tel: (01) 143123
Finland (Helsinki): tel: 642509
France (Paris): tel: 705-6410
West Germany (Bonn): tel: 0228-218095/6
India (Delhi): tel: 601601/5
Indonesia (Jakarta): tel: 512309
Italy (Rome): tel: 805306
Japan (Tokyo): tel: (03) 452-7611/9
Malaysia (Kuala Lumpur): tel: 482177
Netherlands (The Hague): tel: 070-520621
New Zealand (Wellington): tel: 739073
Norway (Oslo): tel: 562211

Philippines (Metro Manila): tel: 817-827
Portugal (Lisbon): tel: 777176
Singapore: tel: 2561188
Spain (Madrid): 4100053
Sweden (Stockholm): tel: 08/16-04-80
Switzerland (Bern): tel: (031) 431081/2
Thailand (Bangkok): tel: 234-0723/6.
United Kingdom (London): tel: (01) 581-0247/9.
United States (Washington DC): tel: (202) 483-7383.

KOREAN FESTIVALS AND HOLIDAYS

New Year Holiday, January 1-3. Many Koreans, however, still save their best food, wine and clothes for Lunar New Year, which occurs some weeks later.

Independence Movement Day, March 1: marks the March 1, 1919 Independence Movement.

Arbor Day, April 5: tree-planting jamboree.

Buddha's Birthday, 8th day of 4th lunar month, usually early May. See "Religion" in "Culture of Korea" chapter, above, for a description of the festivities.

Children's Day, May 5: the day for children to be dressed up and taken on excursions.

Memorial Day, June 6: commemorating those who died for their country.

Farmer's Day, June 15: not a national holiday, but observed at farmers' festivals in the countryside with folk dancing and music.

Constitution Day, July 17: patriotic ceremonies in major cities mark the anniversary of the promulgation of the Constitution on July 17, 1948.

Liberation Day, August 15, marking the surrender of Japan to the Allies and Korea's subsequent release from the colonial yoke.

Chusok, 15th day of 8th lunar month, usually mid-September: Korea's ancient harvest thanksgiving festival. After win-ing and dining, families proceed to hillsides and lake-sides to watch the rising of the harvest moon, the biggest of the year.

Armed Forces Day, October 1: marked by parades and other displays of military pageantry. Major ceremonies are held on the broad plaza on Yoi Island, just south of central Seoul in the Han River.

National Foundation Day, October 3: Also known as Tangun, this holiday commemorates the mythical founding of Korea by Tan-gun in 2333 BC. The ceremonies take place on the summit of Mt. Mani on Kanghwa Island, where the event was supposed to have taken place.

Han'gul Day, October 9: Celebrates the invention of *han'gul*, the Korean alphabet, by King Sejong. Ceremonies at his tomb mark the day.

United Nations Day, October 24: commemorates U.N. soldiers who died defending the south during the Korean War.

Christmas Day. Celebrated throughout the country by Korea's eight million Christians.

Annual festivals

Tongshin-je, 15th day of 1st lunar month; usually around mid-February. An ancient festival related to Lunar New Year festivities and shaman fertility rites; today observed only in remote rural areas.

Unsan Village Ritual, April: A 12-day festival held at a shrine southwest of Unsan Village, Chung- chongnam-do Province, in honor of the local spirit of the mountain. Intangible Cultural Asset No. 9.

Hanshik, 105th day of lunar calendar (March or April): *Hanshik* means "cold food," and in the old days people were not supposed to light fires on this day. Nowadays *hanshik* is an occasion to visit, pay respects to and tidy up the graves of one's ancestors.

Chunhyang Festival, 8th day of 4th lunar month, usually early May: held on the same day as Buddha's Birthday, this festival, at the town of Namwon, Chollapuk Province, celebrates Chunhyang, Korea's favorite heroine, who supposedly lived here. See **Namwon (Off the Beaten Track)** for details of her story. The festival features contests of *pansori*, a form of recitation which originated in the area.

Arang Festival, May 9: Held at Milyang village in Kyongsangnam Province, this festival celebrates the conjugal fidelity of Arang, a popular heroine of the Shilla dynasty. A "Miss Arang Contest" is featured: besides being pretty, the winning girl must demonstrate her skill in literary composition, classical music, calligraphy and embroidery.

Tano (spring) Festival, 5th day of 5th lunar month, (usually in May): Originally an occasion to pray for good harvests, this is a big event in many country towns and villages, with dancing, wrestling matches, swinging contests and shamanistic rituals. Designated Intangible Cultural Asset No. 13, the festival goes on for a whole week in the otherwise somnolent east coast town of Kangnung. In Seoul it is marked with folk dances and shaman ceremonies on the banks of the Han River.

Mahan Folk Festival, October 8: A local festival held in the vicinity of Iksan village in Chollapuk Province, celebrating the history and legends of the Paekche Kingdom. Andong Folk Festival, September 28: Held near the ancient Confucian Academy outside Andong, this festival falls on Confucius's birthday. It features Chajon-nori, "War of Dragons", Intangible Cultural Asset No. 24, in which warriors mounted on monstrous A-frames supported by dozens of burly men strive to throw each other to the ground. Other events include a mask-dance drama and a bridge-crossing game. For more about the archaic town and environs of Andong, see **Off the Beaten Track**.

Shilla Cultural Festival, October

8-10: One of Korea's brightest, most exuberant festivals. Held in and around Kyongju and celebrating the history and achievements of the Shilla Period, events include classical music at Anapchi Pond, a farmers' folk music contest, archery, wrestling and Buddhist dancing. Flags and lanterns bring the streets of the town to life. One of the must-sees of an autumn trip to Korea. If you plan to stay in the town, make your hotel reservation early.

Paekche Cultural Festival, October 13: Puyo and Kongju's answer to Kyongju's festival, described immediately above. The festival honors the great kings and heroes of Paekche, including the 3,000 palace ladies who hurled themselves to their deaths from Falling Flowers Cliff. See **Off the Beaten Track** for more about this area and its history.

Moyang Castle Festival, 9th day of 9th lunar month, mid-October: Moyang Castle was constructed in 1453, exclusively, it is said, by women, and the festival commemorates the achievement. Thousands of colorfully-dressed women parade along the castle walls.

Other activities include singing contests and archery matches.

Halla Cultural Festival, October 18-20: Cheju's annual celebration of its special legacy and identity, the festival begins with the ringing of bells and blowing of whistles throughout the island. Events include art exhibitions and performances of traditional music.

Kaechon (National Foundation) Arts Festival, 3rd day of 10th lunar month (mid-November): Held at the town of Chinju, Kyongsangnam-do Province, the festival is famous for its sword-dance, performed by half-a-dozen dancers accompanied by drumming. Contests and exhibitions of calligraphy and landscape painting, poetry, music and traditional drama are among the other events.

MISCELLANEOUS TIPS

TIPPING

Tipping is not the custom in Korea, and just about the only situation where it is

Interior of Seoul National Museum, recently re-opened in the Capitol Building after extensive refurbishment.

expected is in the *kisaeng* house, where quite large tips are left for the ladies responsible for the entertainment. Taxi drivers do not require tipping unless they carry your bag, but it is common practice to let them keep the change when the sum involved is small.

INTRODUCTIONS AND SURNAMES

Korean forms of introduction approximate closely to Japanese ones. The individual introduces himself, bowing slightly and presenting his name card with both hands - giving anything with just one hand is considered impolite.

Korean surnames were borrowed some 2,000 years ago from among China's "Old Hundred Names." It seems, however, that only about half a dozen of the Old Hundred appealed to Koreans, for millions of them today share a handful of surnames. Given names therefore assume a disproportionate importance, and when you strike up a friendship with a Korean it is a good idea to commit all his or her names to memory. As in China, surnames always precede given names.

The most common surname in Korea is Kim, which means "gold", followed by Lee ("plum") and Park ("white"). Women retain their maiden names after marriage, so don't be taken aback when Mr Kim introduces you to his wife, Mrs Lee.

GEOGRAPHICAL TERMS

The following terms appear as suffixes after place names in maps, brochures and guides; a familiarity with them will help you to make an intelligent guess about the size of the place being discussed:

-*do*: province
-*si*: major city or large town
-*up*: town

-*kun*: major district
-*myon*: township or village
-*ri*: residential sub-district
-*no*, -*ro*, -;*o*: road or street
-*ka*: subsection of road or street
-*gu*: major ward of large city
-*dong*: precinct of a large city, subsection of a ward.

LOST AND FOUND

If you lose something valuable in Seoul contact the Lost and Found Center, Citizens' Room, Seoul Metropolitan Police Bureau, 24-17-4 Namdaemunro, Chung-ku. Tel: 28-9900. You might also tell the Munhwa Broadcasting Co. (tel: 74-6151, 74-2601) and the Tongyang Broadcasting Co. (tel: 23-1211, 28-8211) about it. They may oblige by broadcasting a description of the missing item.

BUSINESS HOURS

Official business hours are 9 am to 6 pm Monday to Friday, 9 am to 1 pm Saturdays. Between November and March clocking-off time is 5 pm. Many private businesses stay open deep into the evening.

Banking hours are 9:30 am to 4:30 pm Monday to Friday, 9:30 am to 1:30 pm on Saturdays.

Most department stores open from 10:30 am to 7:30 pm, with one day off a week. As stores take different days off, you will usually find several open on any day. Sunday trading is universal.

KEEPING CLEAN AND TRIM

A bath-house is *mogyok-tang*; a barbershop is *ibalso*. In Korea both are as much a treat as a utility.

The Korean public bath is very similar to the Japanese. Soaping and scrubbing take place outside the large communal tub, and prior to getting in it.

Some baths also have saunas and a corner to take a nap in. They are open for business from early in the morning to around 8 pm.

Besides the basic hair cut, Korean barbers routinely provide manicure, cut-throat shave and scalp massage as well, and sometimes three or four assistants will be busy with a different part of you at once. Other free extras may include ear-cleaning, hot towels, facial creams, pedicures, and complimentary cigarettes and tea - all good reasons for staying in Korea long enough to let your hair grow.

THE ROMANIZATION MESS

Roman orthography in modern Korea might be compared with the situation in Shakespeare's England, where the Bard himself wrote his own name nine different ways. This is because two drastically different systems of romanization are in use, the McCune-Reischauer, which enjoys international recognition, and the Ministry of Education's system, which does not. Faced with these perplexities, most people (including most Koreans, who have little cause to write their own language in Roman letters anyway) tend to improvise according to the way the word sounds to them. This is weird at first, but after a while you may start to enjoy it; there is an odd sense of liberation in being able to spell any way you fancy.

This is how some important place-names come out in the two different systems:
McCune-Reischauer~Ministry of Education
  Pusan~Busan   Cheju-do~Jeju-do
  Chongno~Jongro Kyongju~Gyeongju
  Sorak-san~Solak-san

In common with most English language guides, we have used the McCune-Reischauer system in this book, with the exception of some names of people where the individuals concerned

have their own preferred Roman form, and the name of the capital, which McCune-Reischauer would spell "Soul".

The only thing to be said for the existence of these two systems is that they do, taken together, help to do justice to the unfamiliarity (to Western ears) and subtlety of Korean pronunciation. Below is a guide to the values of those Korean sounds, as expressed in McCune-Reischauer romanization, which differ substantially from English ones.

l/r: used interchangeably in Korean; no clear distinction made.
a: like *a* in *car*.
ya: like *ya* in *yard*.
o: like *u* in *under*.
yo: as in *York*.
u: like *oo* in *boot*, but shorter.
yu: like *you* but shorter.
u: like *u* in *put*.
i: like *ea* in *eat*, but shorter.
ae: like *e* in *wed*.
yae: like *ye* in *yesterday*.
e: like *a* in *aid*.
ye: like *ye* in *yet*.
oe: like *oeu* in French *oeuf* but shorter.
wi: like *wi* in *win*.
ui: like *wi* in *win*, but without lip-rounding.
wa: like *wha* in *whack*.
wo: like *whu* in *whump*.
wae: like *we* in *wear*.
we: like the first vowel sound in *wait*.

INSTANT KOREAN

Numerals:

1 *Il*		2 *Ee*	
3 *Sam*		4 *Sa*	
5 *O*		6 *Yuk*	
7 *Ch'il*		8 *Pal*	
9 *Ku*		10 *Sip*	
11 *Sipee*		20 *Ee-sip*	
30 *Sam-sip*		40 *Sa-sip*	
50 *O-sip*		60 *Yuk-sip*	
70 *Ch'il-sip*		80 *Pal-sip*	
90 *Ku-sip*		100 *Paek*	

What is that? *Jogosun muo-simnikka?*
That is good *Cho sumnida*
That is bad *Nappumnida*
You are beautiful *Tangsinun yepum-nida*
I like you *Tangsinul joa-hamnida*
Please bring me some... ...*chom kata chu-seyo*
Please give me... ...*chusip-siyo*
Do you have...? ...*iss umnikka?*
How much does it cost? *Olma imnikka?*
It is too expensive *Nomu ppisamnida*
Can you give a discount? *Discountu-rul hal-su-iss- umnikka?*
Can you speak English? *Yong-o hal-su-iss-umnikka?*
How long does it take to get there? *Ol-mana kolimnikka?*
Please stop here *Sewo chu-seyo*
What is this place called? *Yogi-nun odi imnikka?*
Never mind *Kokjong maseyo*

Food and beverages
Korean food *Han chong sik*
beer *Maekchu*
This is delicious *Aju masi sumnida*
Please bring the bill *Kesanso-rul chusip-siyo*
Restaurant *sik-tang*
Bar *sul-jip* Tearoom *Tabang*
For more food and beverage words, see relevant section in **The Culture of Korea**.

Places
Department store *Paekhwa-chom*
Duty-free shop *Myonse-chom*
Local market *Sijang*
Airport *Konghang*
Seoul railway station *Seoul-yok*
Entrance *Ipku*
Exit *Ch'ulku*
Restroom *Hwajang-sil*
Bank *Unhaeng*
Hotel *Hotel*
Good Korean inn *Cho-un yogwan*
Post Office *Uche-kuk*
Police station *Pach'ul-so*
Public telephone *Kongchung-chonwa*

200 *Ee-paek*   300 *Sam-paek*
846 *Pal-paek-sa-sip-yuk*
1,000 *Ch'on*   2,000 *Ee-ch'on*
5,729 *O-ch'on-Ch'il-paek-ee-sip-ku*
10,000 *Man*   20,000 *Ee-man*

Greetings and other civilities
Good morning/afternoon/evening *An-nyong ha-simnikka* or *Annyong haseyo*
Hello (eg. on telephone) *Yobo-seyo*
Yes *Ye*
No *Anio*
Excuse me *Sille-hamnida*
Thank you *Kamsa-hamnida*
You're welcome *Ch'onman-eyo*
Sorry *Mian-hamnida*
See you again *To mannap-sida*
What is your name? *Irumi muo-simnikka?*
My name is... *Na-ui irumun...imnida*
Just a moment, please *Cham-kkan man kitari-seyo*
I beg your pardon *Tasi malsumhae chu-seyo*

Phrases and sentence patterns
Where is...? ...*odi iss-umnikka?*

ABOVE Masks used in rural festival in Kosong province.

Subway *Chi-hach'ol*
Terminal *Chongjom*
South Gate Market *Namdae-mun sijang*
East Gate Market *Dongdae-mun sijang*
Sejong Cultural Center *Sejong mun-wha-hoekwan*

Sample sentences
Where is the restroom? *Hwajang-sil odi iss umnikka?*
Please bring me some beer? *Maekchu chom kata chu-seyo.*
Do you have coffee? *Kopi iss-umnikka?*

Suggested further reading

There is not an embarrassment of good books in English about Korea (though there are not a few that are quite embarrassing). Here is a brief selection of volumes which are helpful or interesting or both.

A New History of Korea by Ki-baik Lee, Cambridge, Mass., Harvard-Yenching Institute/Harvard University Press, translated by Edward W. Wagner and Edward J. Shultz, 1984. Readable and authoritative single-volume history by top Korean scholar.

Koreana by Peter Hyun, Seoul, Korea Britannica, 1984. A profile of Korea's history and culture, dependable if a little stolid. Heavily illustrated with color photographs.

A Handbook of Korea, ed. Kim Young-kwon, Seoul, Seoul International Publishing House, 6th Edition, 1987. Useful almanac for those who want to know *lots* more.

Korea's Cultural Roots, Dr Jon Carter Covell, Elizabeth, New Jersey/Seoul, Hollym International Corp., 1981. A chatty ramble through the traditional culture by this inexhaustible and gleefully controversial scholar and longterm resident.

Korea's Kyongju, Edward B. Adams, Seoul, Seoul International Publishing House, 1979. Difficult to use as a guide, but indispensable for anybody with a serious interest in Kyongju.

Five Thousand Years of Korean Art, San Francisco, Asian Art Museum of San Francisco, 1979. Catalogue of the famous exhibition, with an enlightening introduction and many marvelous plates.

Fragrance of Spring, Chai Hong Sim, Seoul, Po Chin Chai, 1970. Charmingly ingenuous English version of Korea's favorite love story.

Inside Seoul: The Honam Oil Guide to Seoul, Seoul, Benedict Press, 1985. Highly detailed, very practical guide to Seoul, aimed particularly at resident foreigners, with dozens of brilliant maps. Information on everything from jogging to pizza, from taxidermists to plastic flowers.

Korea and Taiwan: A Travel Survival Kit, Geoff Crowther, South Yarra, Lonely Planet Publications, 1982. Practical though far from comprehensive budget guide to the country. Good on the nitty-gritty (cheap restaurants, bars, inns) like all Lonely Planet titles.

Index

1988 SEOUL OLYMPIAD (September 17 to October 2 1988)

SPORT / DATE	Sept 17 Sat	18 Sun	19 Mon	20 Tue	21 Wed	22 Thu	23 Fri	24 Sat	25 Sun	26 Mon	27 Tue	28 Wed	29 Thu	30 Fri	1 Sat	2 Sun
Opening ceremony	•															
Archery												•	•	•	•	
Athletics							•	•	•	•		•	•	•	•	•
Basketball	•	•	•	•	•	•	•	•	•	•	•	•				
Boxing		•	•	•	•	•	•	•	•	•	•	•			•	•
Canoeing										•	•	•	•	•	•	
Cycling	•		•	•	•	•	•	•	•							
Equestrian sports		•	•	•	•	•	•	•	•	•	•		•	•		•
Fencing				•	•	•	•	•		•	•	•	•	•		
Football	•	•	•	•	•	•		•	•		•			•	•	
Gymnastics		•	•	•	•	•	•	•	•			•	•	•		
Handball				•		•	•	•	•	•	•	•	•	•	•	
Hockey	•		•	•	•	•	•	•	•	•	•	•	•	•	•	
Judo							•	•	•	•	•	•	•	•	•	
Modern Pentathlon	•	•	•	•												
Rowing	•	•	•	•	•	•	•									
Shooting	•	•	•	•	•	•	•									
Swimming	•	•	•	•	•	•	•	•								
Diving									•	•	•	•	•	•	•	•
Synchronized swimming									•	•	•		•		•	
Water polo			•	•	•		•	•		•	•					
Table tennis			•	•	•	•	•	•	•							
Tennis				•	•	•	•	•	•	•	•	•	•		•	
Volleyball		•		•	•	•	•	•	•	•	•	•	•	•	•	•
Weightlifting			•	•	•	•		•	•	•	•	•				
Wrestling			•	•	•	•	•			•	•	•	•	•		
Yachting				•	•	•	•			•	•	•				
Closing Ceremony																•